THE

# SOUTHERN WA

## CONTENTS






ISBN 978-1-906419-13-4

First published in 2009 by Kevin Robertson
under the **NOODLE BOOKS** imprint
PO Box 279
Corhampton
SOUTHAMPTON
SO32 3ZX
www.noodlebooks.co.uk

Printed in England by
Ian Allan Printing Ltd
Hersham, Surrey

SOUTHERN
173

SHUNTING
BELL

SWANWICK

# Editorial Introduction

One of the privileges of being able to compile 'SW' is being able to indulge a whim when it comes to the selection of items to be included.

In an ideal world everything would be neatly pigeon-holed and cross referenced and indeed that is the intended theory, so that if I need to search for a photograph on a particular topic it should be in a file marked accordingly. That at least is the intended theory. I also keep together items which have been loaned by others, the only trouble being that one item from that collection is no doubt what sticks in the mind, but other gems could well lurk underneath.

Such was the case with this issue, for when searching for the item on Guildford Station Ambulance records - I promise it is nothing like you might first think, see page 88, I came across the plan of Hook Switches, also loaned by Peter Holt and which fits so well with Graham Hatton's article this month.

At this stage I have to say I am very wary about seemingly identifying any particular feature, suffice to say, there is a plan to what goes in to each issue, although I am guilty as the rest when it comes to sometimes deviating from the intended contents.

That said one advantage of a periodical compared with a book is the way it is possible to respond to demand faster than compared with a book. I have been asked on a number of occasions for features on specific topics, I can assure you all are noted, even if nothing is to hand at that particular time.

Thus an appeal at this stage, please do keep your contributions coming. I will freely admit we are indeed short on items relative to the former South Eastern lines, whilst other topics I have been asked to include in future are features on Dover Docks - again South Eastern of course and Crystal Palace High Level.

I am equally sure many of you will have acquired odd items, whether that be files or photographs from times past and depicting scenes from years ago. The internet has allowed so much more to be shared and for this we can all be grateful, but there are still some to do not, for whatever reason, have access to this resource. Please consider then allowing some of this material to appear in print. I will not make a false promise and say immediately, but neither will I do what one other specialist publisher has a reputation for, hoarding and producing little. Elsewhere others have said information is for sharing, very true, I would add, information is also for enjoying.

Now I have an admission, several of you have written and quite correctly taken me to task over the lack of, or limited space, for letters and feedback. That was never the intention and despite the space again being filled this time, I promise in Issue 7 we will make amends. As ever thank you all for your support.

*Kevin Robertson*

**Left:** *For many years, the 'Southern Magazine' included a regular , 'Gallery of Old Timers' feature. Despite the journal not having appeared for close on 60 years, this view would have fitted the bill even then. It is of course Swanwick, on the coast line between St Denys and Fareham, opened on 2nd September 1889. This view may possibly date from that time. For a country station, the complement of persons present would appear excessive and a number must either be staff from elsewhere, visitors, or even those invited to witness the opening. (Any suggestions would be most welcome.) Typical of course is the LSWR fencing, whilst the only thing against the date suggested is the fact the grass bank appears relatively mature. Could it even be the occasion when the line was doubled in 1910? Many thanks to Bob Winkworth for the submission.*

**Previous page:** *Guildford bound from Woking, circa 1948. John Davenport has captured 4-6-2T, No 518 heading south and passing two Adams' tender locos in the yard. On the right hand side is the, now long forgotten, loco servicing facility in the yard, somewhat basic and consisting of an inspection pit and water supply. Beyond, the raised loading bank may well have once held a stock of coal. See also the article on these engines on page 91*

*John Davenport / The Transport Treasury*

**Front cover:** *The problem of drifting smoke on the unrebuilt Bulleid Pacifics was kept under review by the Southern Region and in December 1959 modifications were made to the cowling of Nos 34035 and 34049. Whilst No 34049 was restored to conventional form in February 1960, 34035 was the subject of further alterations resulting in the design seen here, recorded outside the front of Eastleigh Works in early 1960. The style was retained until withdrawal came in June 1963, No 34035 one of the first four 'Pacifics' to be withdrawn in the same month. (The others were 34043, 34055 and 34074.) Views of No 34035 'Shaftsbury' in this form are seldom seen and indeed this is the first colour photograph so far located.*

**Rear cover**: *22nd November 1964 and on a clear, late autumn day modernisation has come to Brockenhurst. A new signalbox has been erected and engineers are in the process of replacing the old wooden gates with lifting barriers. Around this period, it was a scene that was being enacted at countless locations on the Southern Region and elsewhere, the old railway giving way to the new. Notice the former Brockenhurst 'A' box in the background and the even older No 8 Crossing Keeper's cottage alongside. (The South Western Circle produce an excellent booklet on the crossing keepers cottages of the former Southampton and Dorchester Railway.) Of particular fascination has to be the signage associated with the accompanying road works, a strange mixture of the old and the new, including what appears to be a single lens traffic-light. The worded sign on the left could well be said to have a double meaning, although it was no doubt lost on the non railway fraternity.*

*The late John Bailey*

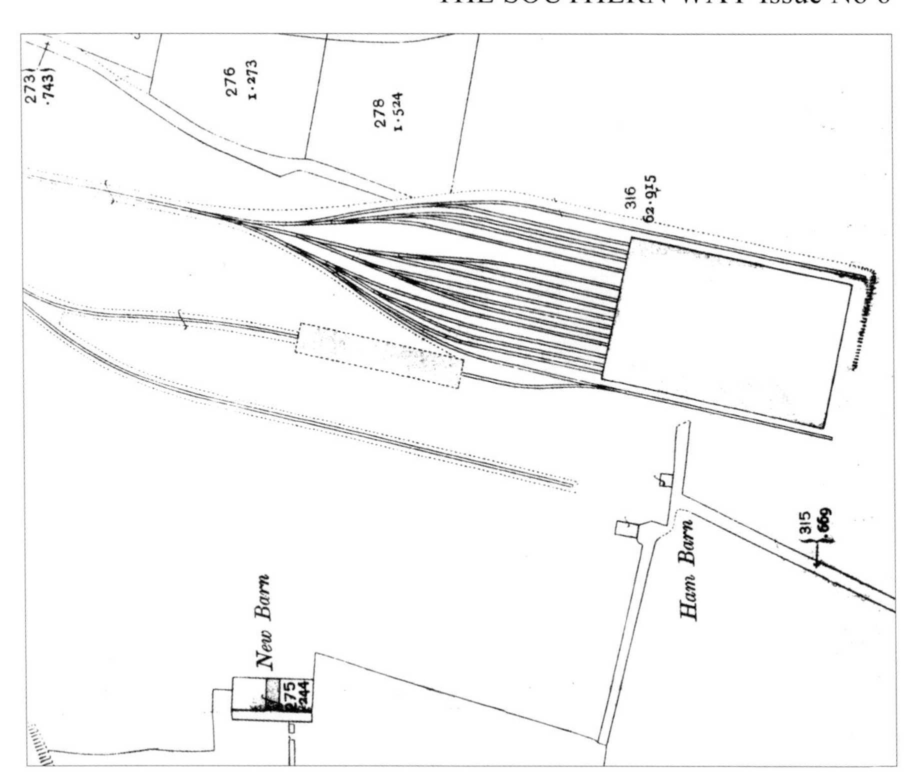


*Schematic diagrams of Lancing Works, 1912 - right, and 1931 - below. Clearly the Paint Shop was the later addition.*

*The Pullman shed, identified from the lower plan, is a slight mystery and may have been specifically provided to service the cars running on the LBSCR and later SR.*

*In the lower plan, the three sidings, continuing lower right, ended a short distance further on.*

*The works firemen's cottages at Bessborough Terrace are indicated at 'A'. Adjoining them is the South Entrance.*

*The coast line runs outside the plan area with the connections from and to the works facing Brighton.*

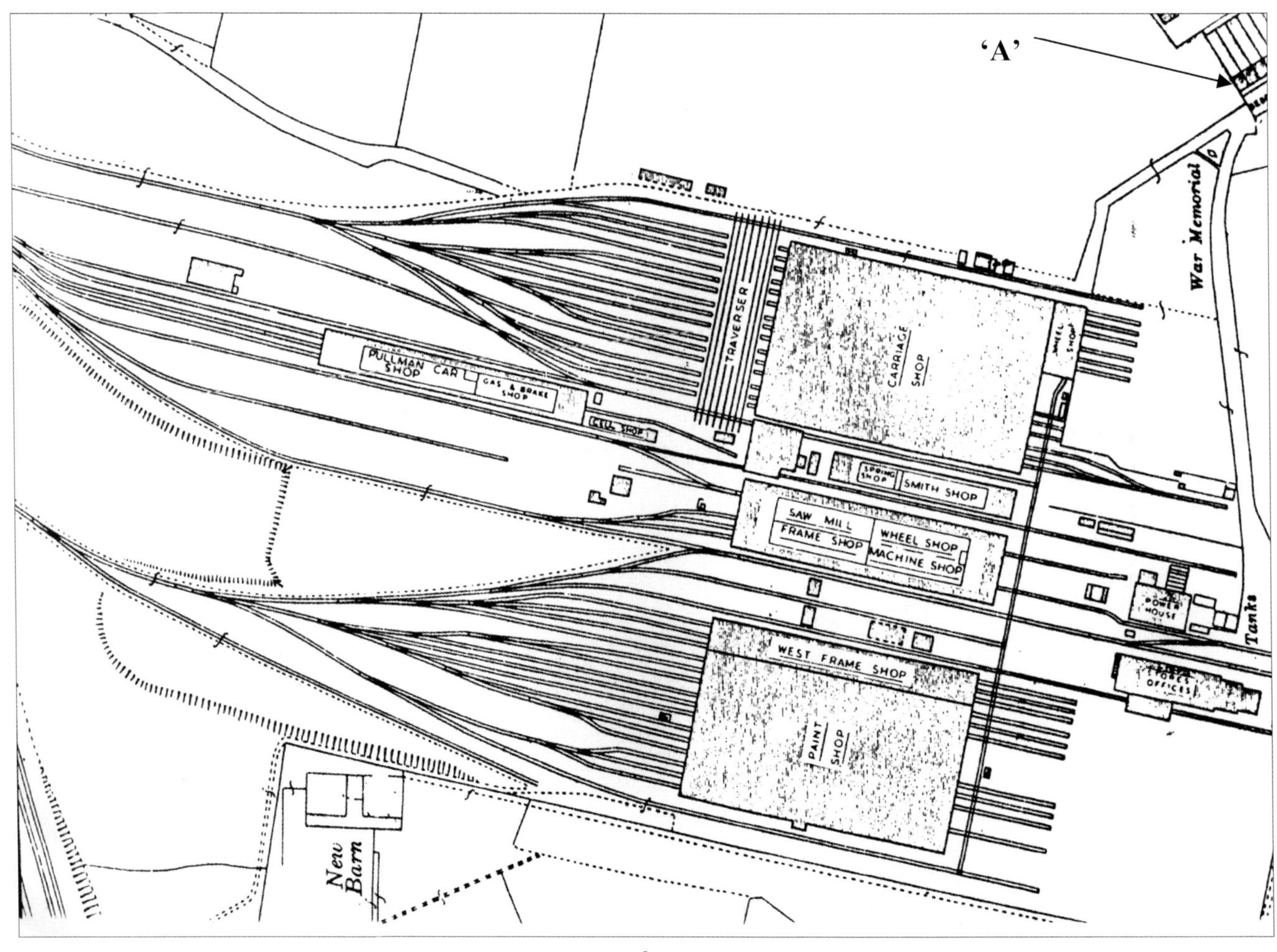

# LANCING CARRIAGE WORKS

## *The first in a series of articles dealing with the former LBSCR / SR Carriage and Wagon Works.*

The history of the carriage works at Lancing is one that has been mainly shunned by researchers. Indeed so far as the Southern and its constituents are concerned, only Nine Elms, Eastleigh and Redbridge have had published works describing their origins, whilst Brighton is recorded only in so far as workers reminiscences relative to a specific timescale are concerned.

This leaves, Ashford and Lancing 'in the cold' so to speak, although it must be admitted that both have been the subject of privately published and circulated records, in the case of Lancing, the work of John H Blackford and Jerry Ames. It follows that no attempt at briefly recording the history of Lancing would be possible without reference to their work 'Railway Recollections. A Memento of Lancing Carriage and Wagon Works'. Another invaluable source is the typed notes of the late Ted Knight, which have been quoted at intervals, suitably abridged.

The works at Lancing owe its origins to a 1902 decision by the LBSCR to establish its carriage works there. Accordingly 137 acres of land were purchased on the south side of the line, east of the existing station, the cost recorded as £21.683 2s 6d.

The decision of the LBSCR to establish a works at Lancing was made to ease the pressure on what were already cramped facilities at Brighton. Up to this time all construction and repair work for locomotives and rolling stock had been carried out at Brighton, but as has been reported elsewhere, inadequate space had led to long delays in repairs being undertaken leading to poor availability of both locomotives and rolling stock. Also expansion of the site at Brighton was also not possible, hence the intention to transfer just wagon building and construction to the new facility, along with the building of horse drawn vehicles.

Evidently the situation at Brighton must have deteriorated rapidly, as just four years later in 1906, Lancing was being described as a 'Carriage and Wagon Works', although at the time still supplementary to Brighton. It's status would increase still further in 1910, when all carriage work was transferred to the new site.

This of course also meant that a number of tradesmen were transferred. For some this meant a transfer of home, a none too popular move, as Lancing, even though it was just 10 miles west of Brighton, lacked mains sanitation and the luxury of piped gas. A lack of suitable housing accommodation near the new works also meant that a number of staff were forced to commute daily, this led to the running of a works service each way daily, later to become known as the 'Lancing Belle'. No similar service ever operated for workers arriving from a westerly direction and who then use a service train instead. (Another railway workers train, nicknamed the 'Lousy Lou', ran between Brighton and Newhaven for the duration of World War 1.)

Another former member of Lancing staff, Ted Knight, referred to travel on the 'Lancing Belle' and

*Recorded from a southerly position, similar to that marked 'A' on the plan opposite, this is a 1920 view of the rear of the works. Some of the buildings on the right still survive on what is nowadays referred to as the Chartwell Road Industrial Estate.*

*10 ton capacity Open 'A' class wagon. A similar vehicle but to just 8 ton capacity was the first vehicle to be built at Lancing in April 1909.*

although his memories are undated, they may well have applied throughout the running of the train.

"The Belle was unlike ordinary passenger trains as each compartment bore a number and every authorised traveller was assigned a seat in one of the numbered compartments. Thus travel on The Belle was restricted to established staff only and new Belle passes were only issued on the retirement or demise of an old hand. For new recruits it was a waiting game, until the time came for the dubious honour of becoming a Belle passenger. Whilst waiting they walked between Lancing station and the works. I have said "the dubious honour", because The Belle was classified in all working timetables as 'third class goods' thus giving all other rail traffic preference over it's passage, much to the disgust of all aboard when delays occurred on the homeward journey. It is, though, fair to record that travel on The Belle was free, as was the first eight miles of any rail journey for other members of staff."

Ted continues, "The arriving workforce gained access to the works by one of three entrances, South Gate, North gate and from the special train directly into the works yard. The South Gate was the main pedestrian entrance and was located at the north end of Bessborough Terrace, the short terrace leading from the seafront into the works. This entrance was used by both pedestrians and cyclists, most being resident locally. There was also the North Gate, situated at the end of a lane leading from Lancing station into the works. Again this entrance was shared by both pedestrians and cyclists alike.

"This lane is well worth a mention not only because rumour had it that it was part of an old snuggling route running from the sea-shore to Sompting Abbots, still standing on the hillside overlooking Lancing Village. For me, however, the lane winding it's way beneath trees meeting overhead was beautiful, a pleasant green and rural walk so unexpected in a smelly, grimy railway works.

"So it was by way of these two gates that the local travellers from Lancing station made their way to work. It is true to say that the cyclists using the North Gate and lane were never really popular with the pedestrians, in fact an uneasy truce existed between them. Many were the verbal exchanges, but fortunately, I am happy to record, few of the physical variety. At this period in history, the age of the opulent railway worker arriving by car was yet to come.

"The remaining body of workers aboard The Belle were transported into the works yard via a rail link from the main line. The Belle came to rest on the line alongside the time office. It was to this office that all manual workers had to report daily to book in. Each worker was provided with a numbered check, this system remained in use until the final years when an electric 'punch-card' system was installed.

"In these pre-war days the road used by The Belle afforded no platform, so every compartment on the train had a short ladder stowed underneath the seat. When The Belle arrived to disgorge it's passengers, the more agile leapt from the stepboard, the less nimble carefully using the ladder provided. In later years the Belle used a siding with a platform provided.

"Friday was pay-day and at the end of the day's work long queues of workers would form in numerical order at the time-office windows. Each man in turn would hand in his pay slip and in return received from the clerk a small tin, about three inches in diameter and two inches or so deep. On the hinged lid was a brass plate stamped with the mans personal number, inside which, was his week's pay. The money was then pocketed and the tin was supposed to be thrown into a drum. Many tins were purposely thrown wide of this drum, I believe as a gesture of contempt for the system, as this pantomime was enacted outside in all weathers, winter and summer, until the outbreak of war in 1939. The same routine then took place in the comparative comfort of the work-shop. Why, one asks, did it take a world war to induce the management to take a more kinder, more civilized attitude towards it's staff? Sadly, one remembers, small as that tin was, it adequately contained a full weeks pay. In later years pay envelopes replaced the tins."

The original works comprised the following facilities, Carriage Building and Repair Shop; 400' x 250', Wheel Turning and Machine Shop; 200' x 100', a Saw Mill; 200' x 100', Wagon Building and Repair Shop; 400' x 250', Power House; 80' x 49', and a Timber Drying Shed; 400' x 50'. A 1912 plan indicated a single large building occupying the site, but this is unlikely to have been able to accommodate all of the above. Certainly expansion took place later, possibly as early as around 1913-4, for by 1931the area of covered workshop accommodation, as well as the siding accommodation, had more than doubled.

The first new rail vehicle to be built at the site was an 8T open 'A' wagon, No. 715 in 1909.

Some years ago a photograph appeared in the 'Down Your Way' series in the Brighton Evening Argus, and showing what purported to be the interior of Lancing Works in 1914 with rolling stock construction taking place. At least two main line steam locomotives were in the background. The view came with the caption that the locomotives were the works shunters. Some doubt though, must be raised over this, not least because one of the engines would appear to be a brand new member of the 'K' class, hardly likely to have been used for such a lowly activity. It is more likely that the view was within the main works at Brighton, with the timescale suggesting the rolling stock work in progress was associated with contemporary war work. Certainly there is no indication that Lancing ever worked on or had facilities for any repairs to steam locomotives, although there was a Pullman shed for repairs to these vehicles.

First World War work undertaken at Lancing included covered railway vans and presumably other rail vehicles for the War Department, also a number of horse drawn vehicles. It was around this time also that a Works Band was established, no doubt in an effort to boost morale. But the ensemble had disbanded by the mid 1920s.

With the grouping of the companies to form the Southern Railway in 1923, Lancing flourished. What was a modern workshop was now scheduled to undertake the renovation of all bogie carriage stock for the SR, as well as the construction of all new carriage underframes. Carriage bodies, for the present at least, would continue to be built at Ashford and Eastleigh, latter to be concentrated on Eastleigh alone.

This resulted in a further expansion of the site, together with the arrival of around 500 men transferred from Ashford. Initially it was not a happy move, although part of the difficulty was a lack of suitable housing in the area, with the new influx compelled to find lodgings during the week. The eventual result was further housing development, in many cases funded by the Southern Railway.

A further development witnessed the introduction of what was then a radical new method of improving efficiency. Up to this time a gang of men under a charge-hand would have been responsible for the whole of the work on a single vehicle although this could at times lead to certain trades being under employed whilst others were at full stretch. The new system, 'The Progressive Carriage Repair Scheme' was introduced in 1928 and resulted in what may be simply, although perhaps not strictly accurately, be referred to as a production line technique. Shortly after this, in 1929, Ashford ceased carriage building in its own right, although the works there would continue to make some underframes as well as underframe components.

Clearly reorganisation on the scale referred to could not be accomplished overnight. Details of the altered method of working were recorded in *THE RAILWAY ENGINEER* for April 1931.

"The first stage of the reorganisation was the transfer of the Wagon Repairers from the Wagon Building and Repair Shop into one bay of the Carriage Shop, and the conversion of the former shop into the Painting, Finishing and Trimming Shops. At the same time one bay of the former Wagon Shop was partitioned off and equipped for use as an Underframe and Bogie Building Shop.

"Prior to the introduction of the progressive system, it was the practice for the men of each grade to be grouped in gangs under a charge hand, and these groups would carry out the whole of the work pertaining to their trade on a vehicle, the routine being that vehicles were lifted, wheels changed and bogie and underframe repairs done in one of the lifting bays. The vehicle then went to one of the body repair roads for attention to bodywork, and finally to the Paint Shop for interior finishing and trimming and interior and exterior painting. Only vehicles

*This and the opposite page, a batch of vans being made for War Department use during WW1.*

41710
41710

*Further WW1 work, this time the underframes for horse drawn carts - as illustrated on page 15.*

previously allocated to the Central Section were dealt with at that time, whereas at present the whole of the Southern railway steam and electric bogie vehicles are repaired at Lancing Works.

"Again before the introduction of the Progressive System, it was necessary to go very carefully into the costs of each operation on the various classes of stock to be dealt with, and also to see that supplies of all wearable parts were available. From the information obtained as to previous costs, it was found possible to split up the work on vehicles undergoing general or intermediate repairs into a number of stages, and to allocate a definite number of men to each stage. By this means the men are kept continuously employed on one class of work at one particular place. The plan drawing of the main Repair Shop, shows that reading east to west, the tracks are laid out and the work respectively done on each as follows;

No 1 Repairs to bodies, intermediate repairs.
No 2 Repairs to underframes, intermediate repairs.
No 3 Repairs to bogies, intermediate repairs.
No 4 Repairs to bogies, general repairs.
No 5 Repairs to underframes, general repairs.
No 6 Re-bedding of lights, general repairs.
Nos 7-8 Stripping of interiors and burning off, general repairs.
Nos 9-12 Re-fitting of interiors and completion of exterior filling and staining, general repairs.
No 13 Exterior filling, general repairs.
Nos 14-15 Body repairs, general repairs.

"At the south end of No 1 road a space is set aside for the heavy repair of bogie trucks, i.e. work outside the usual run of repairs. Spare bogies are also stacked here to replace such bogies needing very heavy repairs, whilst at the south end of Nos 6,7,8,9,10,11, and 12 roads are situated the vacuum brake cylinder testing plant, the Pipefitter's Shop, the Polishing, Finishing and Trimming Shops. The routine for dealing with vehicles due for general repairs is as follows: - On arrival from traffic each coach is carefully examined, and vehicles are selected in groups so that the work of all departments is carefully balanced. Vehicles equipped with electric lighting have the cells and dynamos removed for thorough overhaul, whilst those requiring the roofs recovered are dealt with in a special shop erected for the purpose on the west side of the main shop. This shop has high platforms running along each side to avoid the use of trestles. The work of recovering roofs is always completed before coaches enter the main shop.

"After the vehicles have been selected and the roofs dealt with as aforementioned, they are placed on one of the stripping roads, i.e. Nos 7 or 8. Here all interior fittings are removed, exterior paintwork burnt off, and preliminary steam and hydraulic test of steam-heating apparatus made. Work is carried out on these roads alternately, one road of coaches being stripped whilst the other is being emptied and refilled. At the present rate of output, viz; 22 general repairs per week, 2 hrs 5 mins. is allowed per vehicle. All the seats and backs taken from the coaches pass to the strippers' benches, where the old upholstery is removed and the horsehair sent to the Hair Carding Room. The frames then pass onto the repairers' bench and on to the trimmers' benches. Here the work is divided so that certain men always carry out the same operations to the seat or back, which then passes on to the next man, and so on, till at the other side of the shop it leaves the benches completed and ready for the vehicle on its arrival at the Refitting Roads. The trimmers' benches are fitted with roller tops to facilitate the movement of the seats and backs from one man to the other.

"The trimmers' material stores, cutting machine and sewing machines are so placed that the material moves forward progressively, viz., from the stores to the cutting machine, thence to the sewing machines and afterwards to the trimmers' benches. The brass fittings removed from coaches are placed in numbered boxes and are despatched to the Brass Shop for repairs, cleaning and lacquering, after which they are replaced in the boxes and sent to the Refitting Roads in readiness for replacement on the vehicles. All the other parts of the interior finish-ing, such as mirror and photo frames, &o., go to the Finishers' and French Polishers' benches for repairs, and are completed ready for replacement on coaches on the Refitting Roads. After completion of stripping, coaches are taken off Stripping Roads No. 7 and 8 and placed on No. 4 Road, where lifters remove centre pin cotters, axleguard straps, lubricating pads and dirty oil. Brake-fitters uncouple main pull rods and take down bogie safety irons. All stripped brakework is sent to the south end of the shop, where parts are examined and gauged up, those passed as fit for re-use going back on vehicles, and the remainder despatched for repairs or renewed as necessary. After the vehicle has been at this position for 2 hrs. 5 min. it is lifted bodily from its bogies and placed on temporary mobile bogies on No. 5 Road, down which road it proceeds at the rate of 6 in. per minute.

**Progressive Work on Bogies and Carriage Bodies.**

"The bogies remain on No. 4 Road whilst the following operations are being performed:
Stage 1 Brakefitters strip brakework, south end bogie.
Stage 2 Brakefitters strip brakework, north end bogie, lifters lift stripped bogie from wheels and place in cleaning tank. The wheels and axleboxes are slung and taken by crane to the south end of the shop.
Stage 3 Bogie in cleaning tank 1 hr. 2½ min.
Stage 4 Lifters lift bogie from cleaning tank and place on mobile trestles, after which they remove side and auxiliary springs.
Stage 5 Riveters examine truck, cut off worn liners and brackets.
Stage 6 Riveters re-rivet new liners and brackets. Lifters

remove top bolster and bolster springs.
Stage 7 Lifters examine bolster links, renew wearing plates, replace top bolster and bolster springs, and replace bearing springs.
Stage 8 Painters black up bogie trucks.
Stage 9 Brakefitters refit brakework. Lifters place bogie on wheels, cramp down, and fit axleguard straps. Brakefitters fix safety irons.
The bogie is now lifted on to No. 6 Road.
During the time the bogies are being repaired on No. 4 Road, the following work is proceeding on the body and underframe of the vehicle:
Stage 1 Pipefitters take down gas reservoirs for testing, or Electricians inspect electric wiring and do necessary repairs. Carriage Fitters and Carpenters overhaul and repair buffing and drawgear and examine underframe.
Stage 2 Brakefitters inspect and clean Westinghouse brake cylinders and triple valves; take down vacuum cylinders (which are sent to the testing bench) and replace with tested cylinders. Painters apply first coat of white to interior.
Stage 3 Pipefitters carry out necessary steam repairs, and repairs to vacuum and Westinghouse brake pipes. Painters apply first coat of buff to interior.
Stage 4 Pipefitters complete steam repairs and replace gas reservoirs.
The vehicle, at a period of 8 hrs.20 min. after it was lifted, is ready for remounting on its own bogies, which are now standing ready on No. 6 Road, and the coach proceeds northward at the rate of 6 in. per minute, during which time the following operations are performed:
Stage 5 Pipefitters charge with gas, and overhaul and test gas lamps, &c., or Electricians connect switch wires at end of coach and test wiring, and replace Duplex fittings.
Stage 6 Painters give second coat of white inside compartments. Bodymakers take out quarterlights.
Stage 7 Bodymakers re-bed quarterlights.
Stage 8 Painters apply second coat of buff inside compartments.
At a similar interval, of time *i.e.,* 8 hrs. 20 min. after the vehicle was put back on its bogies, it arrives at the north end of No. 6 Road of the Lifting Bay and is transferred by traverser to one of the Body Repair Roads, Nos. 14 and 15, down which it passes at the rate of 3 in. per minute, where the following operations were performed:
Stage 9 Bodymakers strip floors; mark and take down doors; strip waist panels; strip bottom quarter panels; strip facias, mouldings and doorway plates, and chop off facias on solid jobs.
Stage 10 Bodymakers splice bottom sides where required; renew floors; fit fillets for steel panels; fit waist panels; pin up split panels; pin up all round.
Stage 11 Bodymakers fit steel bottom quarter panels; fix shell mouldings; fit doorway plates. Painters apply first coat of enamel inside roof.
Stage 12 Bodymakers fix radius and straight mould-ings; fix facias; screw up commodes. Painters grain interior.
Stage 13 Bodymakers piece up facias; plane up old panels; hang and regulate doors; fit striking plates; clean up joints. Painters apply coat of lead colour outside.

"On arrival at the south end of these roads the vehicle is transferred to No.13 Road by means of a tractor, and returns up No. 13 Road at the rate of 6 in. per minute. The work performed on this road is as follows:
Stage 14 Painters apply first coat of varnish to interior.
Stage 15 Painters apply first coat of filling to exterior.
Stage 16 Period for drying.
Stage 17 Period for drying.
Stage 18 Painters apply second coat of varnish to interior, and second coat of filling to exterior.

"On arrival at the north end of No.13 Road, the vehicle is taken out by traverser and placed on one of the Re-fitting Roads, Nos. 9, 10, 11 and 12. These roads are worked alternately, and here the coach is completely finished as regards interior fittings and trimming, also exterior filling and staining, the time allowance being 2 hrs. 5 min. per coach. The steam-heating regulator gear is finally tested under steam on these roads.
At intervals of 12 hr. 30 min. six vehicles, completely refitted inside and filled up and stained ready for rubbing down outside, are taken from these roads to the Paint Shop. The process of painting occupies 11 days; while in the Paint Shop the accumulators and dynamos are refitted, after which the vehicles are removed to the Paint Shop Yard, where brakes are tested, and vehicles thoroughly inspected. After the vehicles have been finally passed, the compartments are brushed out, floors cleaned, rugs laid, and the Traffic Department advised that the vehicles are ready for release into service.

**Intermediate Repairs.**

"Vehicles requiring intermediate repairs, i.e., lifting and varnishing, are selected in a similar manner to those for general repairs, so as to balance the amount of work in each department. These vehicles are placed on a road at the north end of the Carriage Shop for cleaning of exteriors and interiors. This road has platforms on either side to facilitate the work and is fitted with con-nections to the vacuum cleaning plant. At the present rate of output, viz., 23 vehicles per week, a vehicle is taken from the Cleaning Road and placed in No. 1 bay of the Carriage Shop on No. 3 Road every 2 hr. Here the lifters remove centre-pin cotters, axleguard straps, lubricating pads and dirty oil. Brake fitters uncouple main pull rods, and take down bogie safety irons. Painters clean interiors and burn off odd panels. Trimmers and finishers strip damaged parts where necessary.

The vehicle is then lifted on to temporary mobile bogies on No. 2 Road, and proceeds down this road at the rate of 6.4 in. per minute. The bogies are left on No. 3 Road, and the following work is performed:
Stage 1.Brakefitters strip brakework,south end bogie.
Stage 2 Brakefitters strip brakework, north end bogie.

*The completed horse drawn vehicles referred to on page 12. As is often the case, it is not just the subject in question that is of interest, but the background also.*

*Regretfully, whilst views of newly finished wagons and WW1 work have been discovered, no coach views of the period have been found.*

*There is a good selection of later day views of Lancing in hand to illustrate further instalments of this series.*

*A newly completed 20T brake van depicted outside the front of the works. This is similar to, but not the same taken at the same angle, as the view that appeared in 'SR Wagons Vol 2' - OPC.*

Lifters lift bogie from wheels and place in cleaning tank. The wheels and axleboxes are slung and taken by crane to the south end of the shop.
Stage 3 Bogie in cleaning tank 1 hr.
Stage 4 Bogie lifted from cleaning tank and placed on mobile trestles. Lifters remove side and auxiliary springs.
Stage 5 Riveters examine truck, cut off worn liners and brackets. Riveters re-rivet liners and brackets.
Stage 6 Lifters remove top bolster and bolster springs.
Stage 7 Lifters examine bolster links, renew wearing plates where required, replace top bolster and bolster springs, and replace bearing springs.
Stage 8 Painters black up bogie trucks.
Stage 9 Brakefitters refit brakework. Lifters place bogie on wheels, cramp down and fix axleguard straps. Brakefitters fix safety irons. The bogie is now lifted on to No. 1 Road.

While the coach is travelling down No. 2 Road the following work is performed: Stage 1 Trimmers and finishers strip damaged parts where necessary.
Stage 2 Brakefitters inspect and clean brake cylin-ders and triple valves. Painters apply first coat of white to interior.
Stage 3 Pipefitters test steam fittings, and repair vacuum and Westinghouse brake pipes.
Stage 4 Pipefitters carry out steam repairs. Trim-mers and finishers refit interior as necessary.

"At an interval of 8 hr., after the vehicle was lifted on to temporary bogies, it is ready to be lifted back to its own bogies, which are now standing ready on No.1 Road, and the coach passes back up this road at the rats of 6.4 in. per minute, where the undernoted work is carried out:
Stage 5 Pipefitters charge with gas, overhaul and test gas lamps.
Stage 6 Painters apply coat of enamel inside com-partments;
Stage 7 Bodymakers re-bed any defective quarter-lights.

Stage 8 Bodymakers carry out light repairs to body.
The time taken to reach the north end of this road is 8 hours, after which the carriage is taken out by traverser and despatched to the Paint Shop for exterior varnishing, this process occupying four days. The vehicle is now taken to the Paint Shop Yard, where brakes are tested, vehicle inspected and cleaned and released to traffic."

Ted Knight recalled that vehicles categorized with he termed 'slight' or 'varnish' repairs, had, before entering the workshops, to progress along the 'Wash Road' and in their turn undergo an exterior wash down with caustic soda and an interior vacuum clean. Ted's words, "The former might sound a simple enough operation, but try to imagine washing down with no cover from the elements on bitterly cold days when ice had to be broken in the troughs before work could begin and the misery of wet days. As a boy I suffered with chilblains on my hands, I really felt for those men. The protective clothing issued really had to be seen to be believed, made of thick heavy white material with a black line marking it out into large squares. Such was the protective suit, which closely resembled Rupert Bears trousers. It was though a grim necessity, there was no alternative.

"With skilled, semi-skilled and unskilled labour involved at the works, the tasks were graded, as of course were the workers. Heavy, dirty and sometimes unhealthy jobs abounded in the works and obviously fell to the unskilled, while the more palatable passed to the semi-skilled and tradesmen."

**Equipment of the Shops.**

Again from *THE RAILWAY ENGINEER.* "In order to deal with the repair of coaching stock economically, the following appliances have been installed or adapted:
Electric surface type traverser supplied by Rasomes & Rpier, Waterside Ironworks, Ipswich, is placed at the north end of the Carriage Shop. The traverser is 70 ft. in length, and is capable of dealing with stock up to 45 tons. The speed of travel of the traverser with a 45-ton load is 200 ft. per minute.

"The four 20-ton overhead electric cranes, two in each lifting bay, have been equipped with grabs, by means of which coaches can be lifted bodily. Stands are provided for these grabs when not in use. The travelling speed of the cranes is 300 ft. per min. in low gear, 500 ft. per min. in top gear, with, a hoist of 50 ft. per min. and a traverse of 150 ft. per min. These cranes were supplied by the Vaughan Crane Company, Openshaw, Manchester.

"Two cleaning tanks or boshes are provided, one to each bay, of sufficient size to take a complete bogie. These tanks are kept boiling by means of steam pipes situated at the bottom and round the sides; the condensed water from these pipes is returned to the boshes by inspirators. A special feature noted was that the boshes, contrary to the usual practice, are fitted with covers, thus retaining the heat and thereby expediting the cleaning process. The covers are made and fitted in such a manner that they can be easily taken off and replaced.

"The temporary bogies on which coaches are mounted on Nos. 2 and 5 Roads whilst their own bogies are under-going repair are of sufficient height to enable men to work comfortably under the vehicles. A system of flood lighting is installed on these two roads (Nos. 2 and 5). These temporary bogies are fitted with a towing iron which engages in a chain running in a slot in the floor, and by this means coaches are moved steadily down the shop. The gearing actuating this chain also moves the coaches back up the shop, when re-mounted on their bogies, this being accomplished by means of wire ropes passing over a series of pulleys, as shown in the accompanying illustration. The bogies while under repair are mounted on wheeled mobile trestles, and these are hauled down the shop at a speed to correspond with the movement of the coaches. This is done by means of clutches engaging with an endless wire rope, driven from the same set of gearing. The temporary bogies and the bogie trestles have the wheels efficiently guarded and the winding gears are protected against overloading or overwinding.

"Wheeled telescopic air lifts are provided to assist in removing and replacing vacuum brake cylinders. At the south end of the bogie roads a pneumatic cramp has been installed for the cramping down of the bogies so that axleguard straps and bogie safety irons can be refixed.

"The axlebox bosh has an overhead runway with electric hoist block for dealing with the axleboxes. Small wheeled hydraulic jacks are provided for the purpose of removing and replacing axleboxes on journals. The use of these appliances very considerably facilitates the handling of the axleboxes and prevents damage being caused to the journals, as would be almost unavoidable were man handling employed.

"Special high wheeled trestles running on trolley tracks between Nos. 1 and 2 Roads and Nos. 4 and 5 Roads are provided to enable men to enter coaches while on temporary bogies, and lower trestles are in use, running on similar tracks, for coaches when moving back on their own bogies. The whole of the lifting roads are well supplied with air points for pneumatic tools.

"Platforms are erected between all the Stripping, Re-fitting and Body Repair Roads, these platforms having pockets at intervals containing plugs and switches for electric hand leads, and those between the Stripping Roads burning-off gas tubes. The platforms between the Body Repair Roads are specially constructed to facilitate work on the bottom quarter panels. The gearing for hauling coaches on Nos. 13, 14 and 15 Roads is situated beneath the platforms. The coaches are hauled by means of wire ropes.

"Up to the present, wheels have had to be sent to the Wheel Shop (a separate building situated about 150 yds. to the west of the Lifting Bay), but a new shop is being constructed at the south end of the Lifting Roads, and will contain two modern wheel lathes, built by Craven Brothers Limited, capable of dealing with all the wheels. This shop will also contain a smith's hearth and small air-driven hammer for dealing with the repair of ironwork details.

"An appliance of considerable interest is the automatic longitudinal profiling machine supplied by Hancock & Co. (Engineers) Limited, Croydon, this representing the latest development in flame cutting. An important feature of the machine is that it will cut to its entire capacity in one setting from a single template and its cutting length can be increased simply by arranging longer main rails. Any shape desired can be accurately cut at one setting quite automatically, handling costs being thus reduced to a negligible amount. A bogie frame can be finished at one setting in 37 minutes, and a feature of the design is that the carriage has perfectly free movement in any direction by means of ball-bearing wheels of unique design, which ensure frictionless and facile motion.

**Shop Alterations and Output.**

"The output of coaching stock from Lancing Works at the present time is 22 vehicles which have received general repairs and painting, 23 vehicles which have had intermediate repairs and touch up and varnish, two Pullman cars, and some non-passenger-carrying vehicles. Prior to reorganisation and before the repairs of bogie vehicles was concentrated at Lancing, the output of repaired coaches was eight general and two intermediate repairs per week. By the introduction of the present system the time vehicles are out of service for the pur-pose of repairs has been very considerably reduced, and the working conditions have been greatly improved.

"Consequent upon the transfer of new body work to Eastleigh, and the installation of the progressive repairs to carriage stock at Lancing, the Saw Mill was re-organised, the machinery being re-grouped into a space half the size of its previous allocation. The half of the Saw Mill vacated has been converted into an additional Frame Shop with overhead crane and the necessary pneumatic and hydraulic plant. The output of this shop is six underframes with their bogies per week.

"There is also the Frame Shop proper, which is adjacent to the Paint Shop, and is capable of dealing with six frames complete with their bogies per week. A system of overhead runways has been placed outside this shop for dealing with steel members. All the rolled sections are moved forward progressively from the yard to the straightening and cropping machine, on to the saws and drills and assembly. The final finish takes place at the north end of the shop, from whence the underframes and bogies are despatched to Eastleigh or Ashford. This shop is equipped with modern machinery, including Hancock oxy-coal gas, solebar cutting machine, Clifton & Waddell cold sawing machines, hydraulic and pneumatic riveters, cranes, runways, 10-head Wilkins & Mitchell machine for drilling solebars, and 33-spindle drilling machine by the same makers for angle brackets, bent knees, plates and other frame details. In addition there is a Machine Shop and a Smith's Shop.

"Power is generated at the Works by three Diesel engines, viz., one 375 B.H.P. and two 185 B.H.P., all supplied by Mirrlees, Bickerton & Day, of Stockport. Also, there has recently been temporarily installed one Belliss-Morcom generating set, rated at over 800 B.H.P., to cope with the extra loads until such time as suitable supplies of power can be obtained from an outside source.

"The Offices are situated at the south end of the Works. In this building is contained the General Office, Costing Office, Rolling Stock Office, Stores Office and Drawing Office. On the ground floor at the north end of the same building is the General Stores, and on the upper floor there is a large Mess Room with accommodation for staff as well as for workmen."

Ted Knight again, "Tea breaks at this time in industrial history were largely frowned upon by the management of factories and works, it seemed that such things were luxuries not for manual workers. No mid-morning break was permitted at Lancing works. This rule, one felt was hard and unfeeling, as many men and boys had left home early to travel and reach the works for a 7-40am start. However sandwiches and beverages were consumed surreptitiously with one eye cocked for any patrolling foreman. During the afternoon shift the workers fared better, as a ten minute tea break was allowed with tea on sale at a half-penny per mug.

The dining facilities for the midday break were not ideal, granted a large mess room was provided and good wholesome food both plentiful and cheap was on offer, but to be fair many workers, failing to discard dirty, greasy overalls, did little themselves to make the old mess room a gourmets paradise. Most brought sandwiches and opted to dine elsewhere."

*The earliest arrangements for shunting in the works are not known although this particular conversion, a former 'Ford' was in use on some of the sidings until 1934/5.*

**Timber Seasoning Methods.**

*THE RAILWAY ENGINEER* - "Artificial timber seasoning is carried out at Lancing Works in a modern Sturtevant two-compartment drying kiln. The timber is loaded on special trucks outside the compartments and pushed into the kiln ready for drying. When piling the timber, sticks are placed between each layer, so as to ensure the whole surface of the timber being exposed to a current of air. In addition to the drying compartments, a boiler room and control chamber is included in the same building. The latter room contains the following apparatus : —

1. The fan driven by electric motor.
2. Steam coil air heaters.
3. Various controls.
4. Indicating instruments.

The three essentials upon which seasoning depends are:

1. The circulation of air round the timber.
2. The temperature of that air.
3. The humidity of the air.

"By careful manipulation it is possible to obtain ideal conditions for any class of timber. Suitably conditioned air is supplied to each compartment in the following manner: A centrifugal fan driven by an electric motor and connected with the outside atmosphere passes air over steam coil heaters. This air then flows through suitable openings in the distributing duct of each of the two compartments, and through the pile of timber, absorbing moisture and losing heat in the process. The moist cool air leaves the compartment at floor level on the opposite side and escapes through an underground wet air return main into a vertical waste air shaft and discharges into the atmosphere above the roof.

"The principal advantage of this system is that it obviates the necessity of carrying large stocks of valuable timber, as is necessary when natural seasoning by exposure to the weather is adopted. By the system described, any kind or thickness of timber can be quickly brought to the exact conditions required for its particular purpose, and batch after batch can be seasoned to the same degree with unfailing regularity.

**Some General Details.**

"The Southern Railway, Chief Mechanical Engineer's Department, Lancing, has, for fire protection purposes, its own private brigade of twelve men, who are housed in a terrace immediately outside the south entrance to the works. The twelve houses are each, connected to a fire alarm apparatus (electric), and, should the necessity arise, the watchman from various convenient points inside the works can ring all firemen simultaneously. On entering the works, the drop indicator inside the south gate shows by disc the position of the fire. The bells continue to ring until the disc is replaced. Placed at useful points in and around the shops and timber stores, &c., are 72 hydrants for high-pressure water. In May, 1929, a Merryweather's "Hatfield" trailer motor pump was obtained. This is capable of delivering 250 gallons per minute. The hose is fitted with instantaneous coupling.

"For protection against oil or petrol fires (where water is useless), a 34-gallon normal capacity "Foamite" firefoam chemical engine, supplied by Foamite Firefoam Limited, is maintained. This is also of the trailer type, and, like the motor pump, can easily be hauled to the necessary point. This engine is capable of generating approximately 300 gallons of foam, which by its own pressure of generating can be thrown about 50 ft. In addition, and for dealing with small or incipient fires, several "Foamite" and "Phomene" extinguishers of either one or two gallons capacity are placed in the various shops. "Pyrene" extinguishers are also to be found in the power house, and at convenient points else-where. As they are of the "Tetrachloricle" type, their primary purpose is for electrical outbreaks, although, as above stated, they are found at various points, and are used when it would be uneconomic to use larger ones."

Perhaps surprisingly, Ted Knight refers to smoking been permitted within the works, "Smoking was however allowed on the shop floor except of course where an obvious fire hazard existed, for example in the sawmills, paint and oil stores and inside any rolling stock. To minimise fire breaking out, a hooter was sounded in every shop one hour before the end of the shift. The idea being that any fire would surely be discovered within that hour. Smoking after this hooter was forbidden, this rule was strictly enforced.

"In retrospect these precautions really worked for in all my service at Lancing I cannot remember a fire ever breaking out."

Finally, from, *THE RAILWAY ENGINEER*, "It will be seen from the foregoing that very considerable improvements have been made, not only in the shops and their equipment, but the main point is, of course, the system of working that has been introduced. This has already, in the relatively short time it has been in operation, been the means of securing considerable economies, and, as it is the constant endeavor of the Chief Mechanical Engineer, Mr. R. E. L. Maunsell, and the Works Manager (Locomotives, Carriages and Wagons), Brighton and Lancing, Mr. G. H. Gardener, to improve still further the methods employed by every means at their disposal, still greater economies may be confidently looked for in the future."

***To be continued.***

# BUDEFUL DRUMMONDS

After several attempt Bude was finally reached by rail on 10th August 1898. The first effort was made in 1965 by the Okehampton Railway, later renamed the Devon & Cornwall. As was quite often the case, raising finance was a problem and the Powers lapsed. The second attempt in 1873 saw authorisation to build from Meldon as far as Holsworthy. Work commenced in 1876 with the 17.75-mile line from a junction with the main line at Meldon opening on 20 January 1879. Holsworthy was to become the Devon & Cornwall's rail head, although by now the line has been leased by the LSWR. A local company obtained powers to extend to Bude in 1893 but failed to make progress. The result was that the LSWR built the line themselves. A luxury coach service provided the missing link until the opening of the line.

The station was rebuilt by the Southern Railway in the 1930s to cater for the ever growing tourist traffic. Nationalisation came with little effect on the SR's lines in Devon and Cornwall. The introduction of BR Standard locomotives was not all that apparent, until they were displaced from other areas with the spread of dieselisation. However, the decrease in freight traffic together with the increase in car ownership during the early 1960s was putting a hole in the finances and following transfer to the Western-Region in 1963 the 28.5-mile line's days were numbered

Rationalisation and dieselisation failed to stem the operating losses and Bude lost its remaining passenger services on 3rd October 1966.

# BUDEFUL DRUMMONDS

When Dugald Drummond took up the reins as Mechanical Engineer of the LSWR in 1895 Nine Elms was constructing 20 'T1' 0-4-4Ts that had been ordered by his predecessor. Although the first 10 were completed with minor modifications, the balance was cancelled on 27th May 1896 and Drummond was authorised by the Locomotive Committee to seek tenders for the supply of 20 large passenger bogie tanks to his own design. The cost was estimated at £1,600 each.

Tenders were received from Robert Stephenson & Co, Kitson, Dübs, Neilson, Beyer Peacock, Vulcan Foundry and Sharp Stewart. None came near the Locomotive Committee's estimate and the order was increased to 25 locomotives to be built at Nine Elms. The first batch, Nos 245-56 and 667-76, entered traffic between February and December 1897 at a cost of £1,580 each. Other orders were to follow until by December 1911 a total of 105 locomotives were in traffic.

The class came to be seen over virtually all of the LSWR's metals during the following 50 years. When introduced the London suburban services were worked by Adams Radials and 'T1' and 'O2' tanks, so as a consequence the first batch of 'M7' was allocated to Guildford. The 5ft 7in diameter driving wheels gave a good turn of speed, with the mid-50s being easily possible. The high speed running was curtailed as a result of a derailment near Tavistock in March 1898 and the class was restricted to suburban and local services. As the LSWR/SR suburban lines were electrified they slowly moved westwards.

The subject of these two photographs, No 35, was delivered from Nine Elms in April 1898 on short frames, not being motor-fitted. Those motor-fitted were of the long-frame type. By 1933 it was allocated to Exmouth Junction and been sub-shedded at Bude where it is depicted. Its duties would have generally been confined to working southwards to Okehampton, returning to Exmouth for routine servicing. Transfer to Plymouth in 1935 would have seen it working services to Tavistock, Brentor and Okehampton.

Nationalisation saw a renumbering to 30035 in December 1948, being repainted into BR lined black livery on the same date. It was shopped at Eastleigh around the same time. It remained a west country engine, shedded at Plymouth until 1960, when it was transferred to Eastleigh, then on to Feltham from where it was withdrawn in February 1963. Storage was at Eastleigh from February 1963 until February 1964 when it was dragged back to Nine Elms en-route to Woods, Queenborough, where it met the gas axe in June 1964.

The LSWR's'K10's could be referred to as an 'M7' built backwards with a tender added, as all the important dimensions were the same. No 152 was constructed at Nine Elms in December 1902, being a modification of the 'C8' class with smaller diameter wheels. Costing an average of £2,085 apiece, the class became known as the 'hoppers', adjusted to 'small hoppers' after the larger 'L11s' entered traffic. Allocated to Exmouth Junction, No 152 would have worked the longer distance services to the West Country resorts. Transfer to Bournemouth then followed before moving to Yeovil, where, in 1939, it was one of five locomotives allocated with only three booked duties. The 'K10s' along with countless other small to medium-sized locomotives were being ousted by larger, more powerful mixed traffic types. Withdrawal would have occurred in the early 1940s except for the intervention of a certain German and, due to postwar material shortages, 31 of the class survived to be Nationalised in 1948. No 152 was not renumbered and was withdrawn and scrapped at Eastleigh in February 1949.

***Contributed***

ASS
INE
FFICE
3025

# HUMAN ERROR AT LONDON BRIDGE?

## ( - OR A SUBSEQUENT ERROR BY THE INSPECTING OFFICER?)

Accidents are a sad yet inevitable feature of railway operation. The various causes are also innumerable, human error, mechanical failure or outside interference, even a combination thereof. Yet, when no other explanation presents itself, it is invariably the driver who will be held to account. This can be especially difficult when that person is himself killed. In the annals of railway history this has been the case in any number of well known accidents, including Salisbury and Moorgate and also, as occurred here, at one of the terminal platforms of London Bridge on the morning of 23rd January 1948.

The circumstances are easily explained, as at 9.35 am, the 8.05 am electric service from Seaford to London Bridge overran the Inner Home Signal at 'on' and collided, at about 15 mph, with an empty passenger service awaiting signals to leave Platform 14. Three fatalities resulted, the Driver of the incoming train, a Passed Fireman travelling with him who was learning the road and an intending passenger, struck by the empty train as it was pushed onto the concourse by the force of the collision. A further 79 persons were injured, three being detained in hospital.

The Ministry Report, conducted by Brigadier C A Langley, affords the usual amount of useful, factual information, although it conspicuously lacks comment concerning other areas which will be referred to later. Firstly, the facts.

The signalling was reported as operating correctly, the weather was fine and the rails dry. No defect was found subsequently in any of the electric units involved. The gradients in the area were referred to as 'negligible' so we must turn our attention to the circumstances in the station itself and also to those of the deceased Motorman.

The empty train consisted of two six-car units, although we can only be certain of the identity of one of the sets, that seen in the illustrations, No 3025. The second six-car set was similar type but included a buffet car.

The approaching train similarly consisted of two six car sets, one we know to have been a 6PUL unit. Although the train was referred to as originating at Seaford, it was in fact two separate services, one from Seaford, the other having started its journey at Ore. Both sets had been joined into one train at Haywards Heath.

We are told that in the driver's cab of the empty set, waiting to leave Platform 14 was Motorman C A Archer. He recalled seeing the Seaford train approach the end of the station at what he described as 'normal speed'. He watched as the train approached him, expecting first that it would divert into Platform 15, on his right and if not, to his left into Platform 13, both of which were empty. The distance from the turnout which would have taken the approaching train into Platform 13, to where Archer was sitting, was around 129 feet. Travelling at 15 mph the approaching service would have covered this distance in about 17.5 seconds. Archer thus did not have long to react. By the time he had realised something was seriously wrong, he had first to leave his seat, open what was an inward facing door and leap to safety onto the platform. Without doubt this action saved his life, as both his drivers cab, and that of the approaching train were crushed back to the guard's compartment in the resulting collision. Under the circumstances it is clear how Motorman E J Watson and Passed Fireman B H Peddlesden lost their lives, trapped in the wreckage.

Motorman Archer recounted at the enquiry that he was certain Watson had been in charge. This was confirmed by the driver of another empty service, Motorman A D Jupp, which had just left Platform 15 and so passed the incoming train on its approach. He was certain that Watson was driving, with Peddlesden observing ahead from the offside. The two men did not appear to be in conversation.

Archer estimated at the time of collision that the impact speed had been reduced to around 10 mph, he also heard Watson shout, but the report makes no mention of what he might have said, but we can imagine. He also believed he had heard an emergency brake application being made - witness the sound of escaping air.

The Guard of the train involved, W G Watmore,

***Left*** *- The aftermath, recorded whilst clearing up operations were still in progress. The angled image was as recorded by the photographer and whilst it would have been an easy matter to straighten, we felt too much detail would be lost in the resulting 'crop'. Platforms 8 - 17 were closed after the collision but Nos 8 - 11 were reopened, partly, by 9.50 am - just 15 minutes after the collision and fully by 11.00 am. The station was fully back to normal at 7.40 pm and whilst this was a rapid feat, it was still reported that 24 trains had been cancelled and the working of 54 others altered.*

***This page and opposite*** - *The remains of the damaged bookstall at the end of Platform 14. Contemporary reports refer to the fact that as well as the assistants, several other people were buried as the structure collapsed. The rear end of the empty train had been driven off the bogie at this end of the motor coach and carried some 23 feet beyond the end of the platform. The bogie referred was also the only set of wheels derailed. No views have been found of the point of impact between the two trains, but with the fatalities that occurred here, that is perhaps not surprising. Interestingly, except at the point of actual impact between the two trains, there was no buffer-locking or over-riding of the buffers. No windows were broken in any of the sets. Contemporary reports of the incident were absent from any of the railway publications of the day. The fact that the situation was cleared quickly and normal service resumed within a few hours was no doubt part of the reason.*

was knocked down by the collision and suffered from shock. Brigadier Langley commented that he was only able to give evidence a month after the collision and even then his recollections of the circumstances immediately prior to impact were 'hazy and not altogether reliable', although he admitted not having seen the indication of the signals as the train approached the terminus.

With the signalling verified as working normally (but see later), the explanation was put forward that Motorman Watson may have confused a clear aspect on an adjacent line as applying to the one on he was on, but this was rejected by the Enquiring Officer.

Where confusion occurs is relative to the signalling and where one of the 'running dummies' was concerned, more accurately shunt signal No 135. According to the signalman, this was correctly showing 'red'. Also the track circuits were checked and found to be working correctly. One ground signal, No 140, was however showing 'green', but this would not have applied to the incoming train. However, when Carriage & Wagon Inspector B Dart, in company with Chief Inspector Nelson and Assistant Scammel were examining the incoming train

15 minutes later, all three were adamant that it was No 135 that was showing 'green'. They stuck to this under cross-examination and were certain they had not confused it for No 140 which was situated further out. Brigadier Langley however, discounted this, on the basis that it was not born out by the signalling equipment and also the observation was made 15 minutes after the accident. He felt that either they were confused or that an unknown person may have subsequently cleared No 135 since the accident.

Had Watson somehow missed the main incoming signal and subsidiary ground signal? Could it have been that Dart and his two colleagues were correct in what they saw they saw and that Watson did see a green light even if he somehow missed the main indication? According to the report, the main gantry, displaying a 'Red' indication would have been visible for a distance of 200 yards. Assuming the incoming train was travelling at 25 mph at this point, it would have been in view to the two men for a little over 16 seconds. (None of these timings are referred to in the report.)

What was not commented upon was Watson's previous record and how long he had been driving trains into London Bridge and even more relevant, what his previous duties had been. Had he, for example, performed the same duty the day before, or during the previous week? We are not told how long he had been working over this route. What we are told is that his personal record was 'Fair', no further explanation being given. Both were experienced railwaymen with many years service behind them His travelling companion, Passed Fireman Peddlesden, was in the cab to 'refresh his route knowledge'. There is no further explanation. How out of date was he, was this his first route-learning trip, or one of many? To be fair, even if Peddlesden had noticed the error being made by Watson and allowing for the fact that no fireman or second-man ever feels comfortable in countermanding a driver's actions, there can surely be little doubt that, if he had been aware of an error such as passing or ignoring a signal, he would surely have shouted out to the effect, "You've just passed a red!" The pronouncement, no doubt, all the more urgent due to the knowledge that in a congested area such as a terminus, the likelihood of other trains being in proximity was proportionately greater. Peddlesden's own personal record was referred to as 'excellent'. Subsequent medical examination of both men revealed no health issues likely

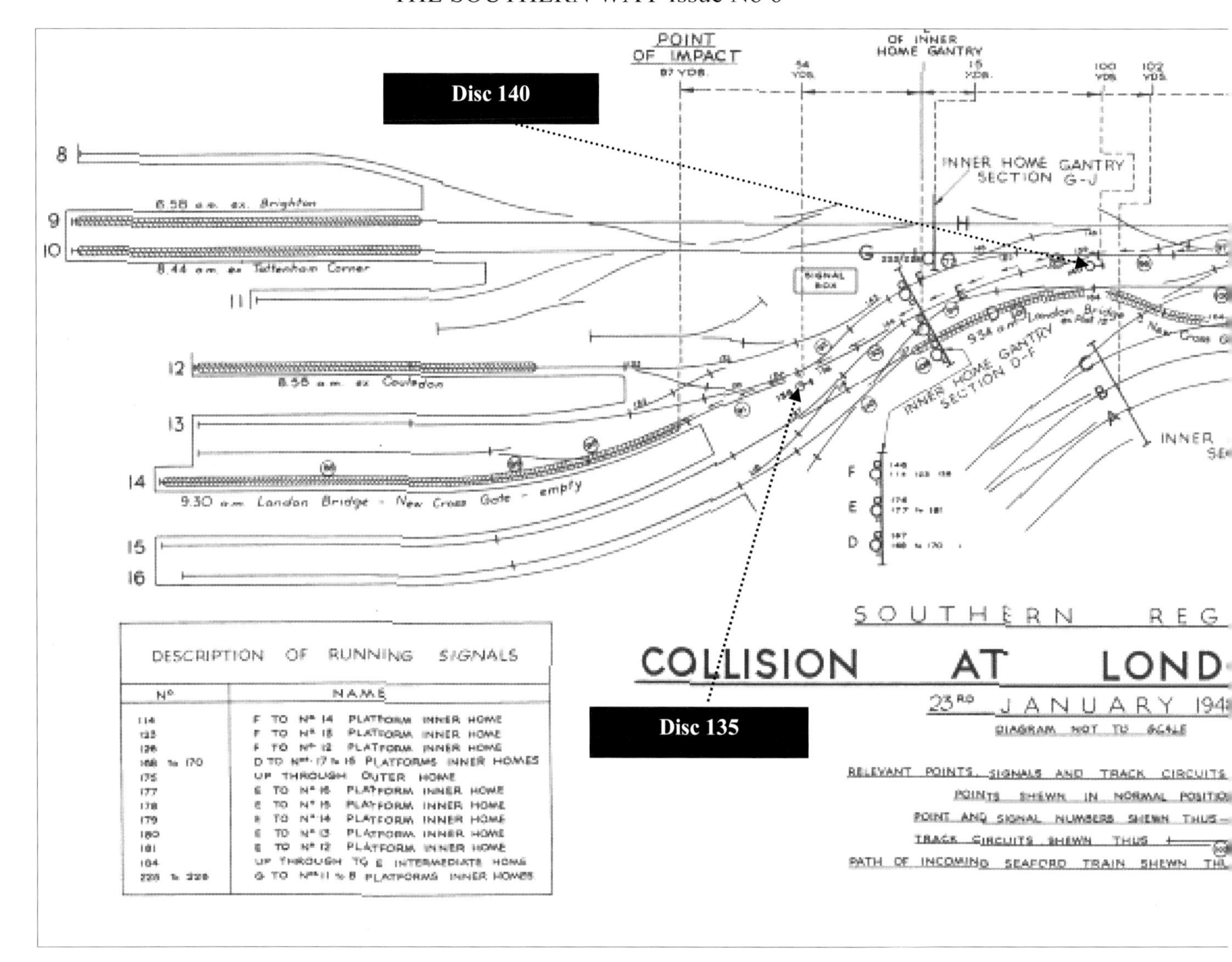


to have affected their judgement.

Speed we know was not an issue, 15 mph was quite normal, although it is a sobering fact that even at what many of us regards as an almost pedestrian pace, the damage caused by the momentum of 509 tons travelling at 10-15 mph is considerable.

The terminal platforms at London Bridge were not provided with hydraulic buffers. This had been considered previously, but it was felt the loss of track and platform length would have made installation impractical. The lack of this equipment no doubt contributed to the damage wrought at the end of the platform as the empty set was pushed up and over the buffers. It was unfortunate that immediately behind the buffers was located a bookstall and that the two employees there were injured as the structure collapsed around them. We may assume also that there was no provision for detonator placing in an emergency as there is no mention of this in the report.

The empty train was also standing with its brakes released, anticipating its own clear signal to proceed, as such the damage and injury potential was spread over a wider area compared with the effect of hitting a stationary train which may well have absorbed part of the resultant energy.

Unfortunately also, as is still common practice, passengers are likely to have been standing up in the approaching train ready to exit at the first opportunity. This then accounted for the 74 passengers and one Pullman employee who were injured on the approaching train, but we are also not told the number of persons who were on the train itself.

So was it a question of driver error, complacency perhaps, or even confusion? Did Watson miss the all important signal or become confused about what he did see? It is hard to believe two men, supposedly both keenly observing the route ahead would make the same error, but without knowing the previous record of Peddlesden over the route it is hard to draw a conclusion. Possibly Brigadier Langley did not mention these points as he simply did not feel they were relevant, but they are relevant and certainly the information, if to hand, would have been easy to ascertain.

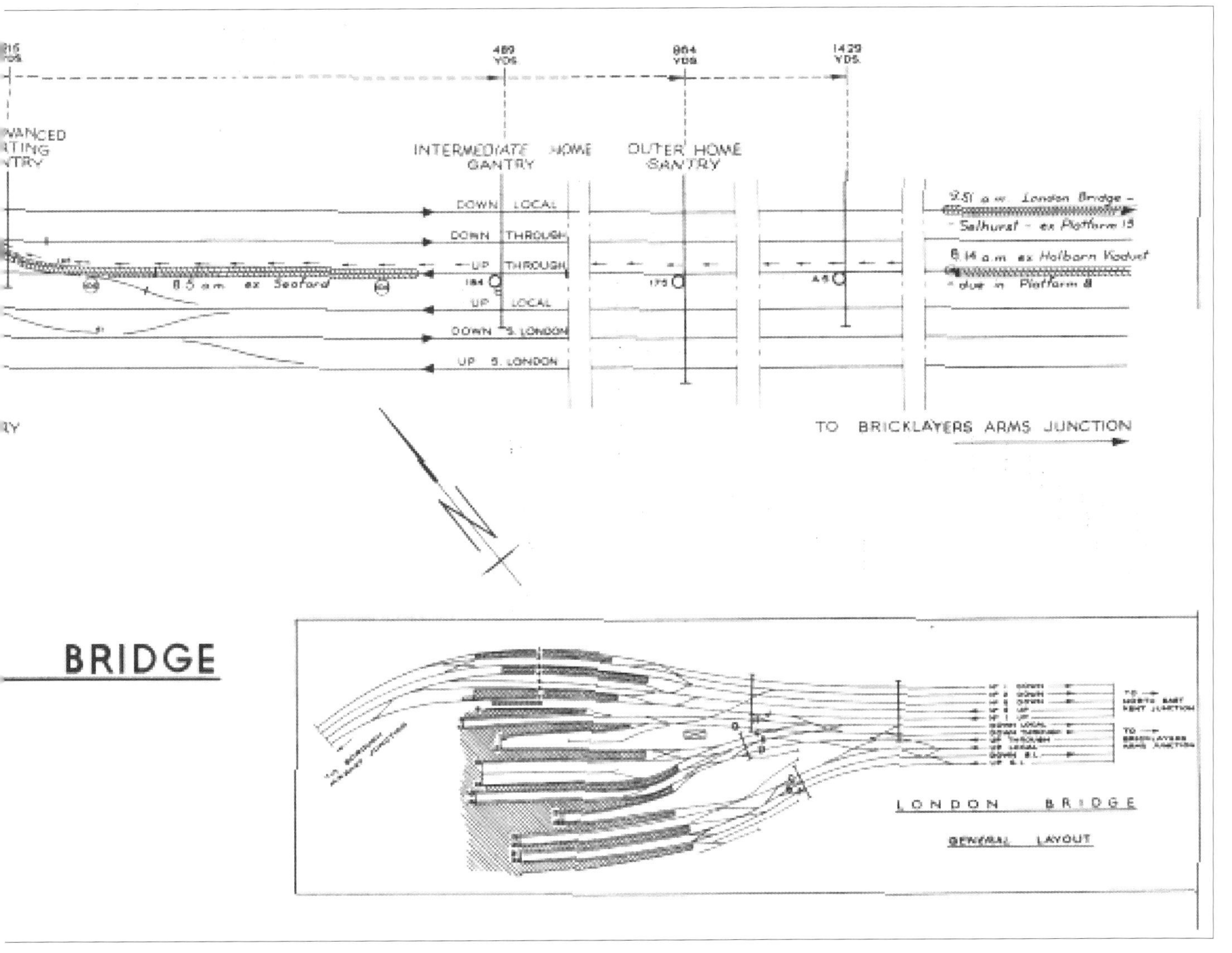


We are left, then, with the conclusion that here is an accident report where it was all too easy to hang the fault onto a deceased member of staff, unable to defend himself. If he was at fault then he paid the ultimate price for a moment of error, certainly there is nothing to suggest that this was a calculated attempt at suicide - especially after the comment made by Archer just prior to impact.

Brigadier Langley in his recommendations makes limited reference to the fitting of hydraulic buffers. In this area the predecessor of the Southern Region, the Southern Railway must bear some culpability. It is all too easy to conclude that this type of accident, or the simpler one of a train colliding with buffers, was rare enough not to warrant the expense involved. Langley hoped that their provision would now be reviewed as the station was even then due for rebuilding following war damage.

He also makes comment over the provision of an emergency escape door, opening away from the cab, back into the guard's compartment. Some sets were already being fitted with this but of a type that the door had to pulled rather than pushed open from the cab area. Even then another problem might have arisen had luggage been placed to block the door opening.

The last omission has to be concerning detonators, where reference is made, and the equivalent of a 'trip-cock' type switch, even then operating on the Underground lines. British Railways had always seemed reluctant to adopt such an item of equipment on their heavily used suburban routes, but here is a case where it would have come into operation immediately the train had passed the inner home signal at 'On'

Instead Langley refers to the fact the men may have been distracted in conversation although this again discounts the evidence given by Motorman Jupp.

So was this human error or could it have been a rogue fault with the signalling as implied by Inspector Dart and his colleagues?

London Bridge January 1948 is not perhaps as clear cut as it might appear. What is more surprising is that these omissions and questions were there to be seen from 28th April 1948, the date the Inspecting Officers report was published. Regretfully no one appears to have asked the questions at the time.

***Top*** *- Without doubt the prestige train passing though the Southampton Control area was the 'Bournemouth Belle', any delay to which would be severely frowned upon. On 18th October 1958, 35017 'Belgium Marine' slows for the stop at Southampton Central with the down working, due at 13.58. The concrete building alongside is 'The dug out', the former control building.*

***Bottom*** *- On 25th October 1958, 34063 '229 Squadron' has charge of the up 'Statesman' boat train having left the New or western Docks and joined the main line at Millbrook. These services, whilst given an allocated pathway, could also run in any one of several 'Q' (spare) paths available, as the arrival and clearance time through customs for passengers and baggage could not be guaranteed.*

*Both: Ron Roberts*

# LIFE AT SOUTHAMPTON TSO

## Richard Simmons

### *Part 1: Introduction and Overview*

So what was the TSO? Its full title was the Trains Supervision Office, but it was generally known as the Control and when this word was pronounced, for some reason emphasis was placed on the first part of the word - con!

The Southern Region (SR) did not have a control organisation similar to other regions and it was generally reckoned by staff that this was a cost cutting measure. On the SR TSOs were staffed by ordinary clerical grades and not controllers, clerical grade salaries being less than those of controllers. As an example of the differences, on the SR it was the duty of the Station Master, often in conjunction with the relevant Area Inspector, to institute single line working (SLW) when required and not the TSO. Neither did the TSO have spare sets of footplate crews to use when required, only motive power depots (MPDs) could provide these. So this article attempts to explain the office's function and some of the types of traffic the railway conveyed at the time and possible problems arising there from.

**We are delighted to include what is the first instalment of at least three parts of recollections into life at the Southampton Train Supervisors Office, 'Control', in the mid 1950s onwards.**

**So far as the enthusiast was concerned, this period has to be the high point of steam working, a time also when the railways not only carried vast amounts of passenger and freight but were similarly tasked with numerous special and excursion workings.**

**Richard Simmons has carefully chronicled his time at Southampton with such detail so as to give a whole new insight into train working, whether viewed from contemporary photographs, a study of track diagrams or perusal of the timetables and special traffic notices of the period.**

**Area of Jurisdiction.**

The Southern Railway divided its territory into sections overseen by Divisional Superintendents, under BR this latter title changed in the early 1950's to District Traffic Superintendents. District offices were, at the time of nationalisation, located as follows: London East at Orpington, London Central at Redhill, London West at Woking, Southern at Southampton Central and Western at Exeter Central. There was also a London District Freight office at Tooley Street, London Bridge. The public timetable denoted London East as the Eastern Section, comprising the former SE&CR. London Central as the Central Section comprising the former LB&SCR. Finally, London West, Southern and Western as the Western Section comprising the former L&SWR.

The Southern, or Southampton, area of jurisdiction was as follows, Basingstoke to Weymouth Worting Junction was the actual district boundary, more also about the Dorchester Jct.-Weymouth section later. Salisbury (Milford Goods) - Cosham (Portcreek Jct. and Farlington Jct.) via Southampton and Eastleigh, Andover Town (Clatford)-Romsey, Alton (Butts Jct.) to Winchester Jct. (Mid Hants line) and Fareham (Meon Valley line), the Fordingbridge line, Brockenhurst to Poole and Hamworthy Jct. via Ringwood (the "Old Road"). Also the following branch lines;- Fareham - Gosport, Fawley, Lymington and Swanage. The former Didcot, Newbury and Southampton line (DN&SR) from Newbury (Enborne Jct.) to Shawford Jct. was also included but as this was an ex-GWR line it was worked under WR regulations between Newbury and Winchester Chesil. The former SR/GWR joint line from Weymouth to Portland and Easton was also a WR regulation worked line. In addition the following freight only branches were also in the division:- Botley - Bishops Waltham, Fullerton - Longparish and Hamworthy Jct - Hamworthy Goods. Sadly many of these lines are long closed.

The Somerset and Dorset (S&D) though nominally part of the Southern Division, somehow managed to preserve a form of independence due to the fact that it was overseen by a sub-office at Bath Green Park. It managed it's own affairs but reported to the Southampton office. As far as the control was concerned, it reported details to us of late running, mishaps and statistics etc. Bath control was, however, a control in the true sense of the word, more in line with other regions' control offices. The S&D also brought into

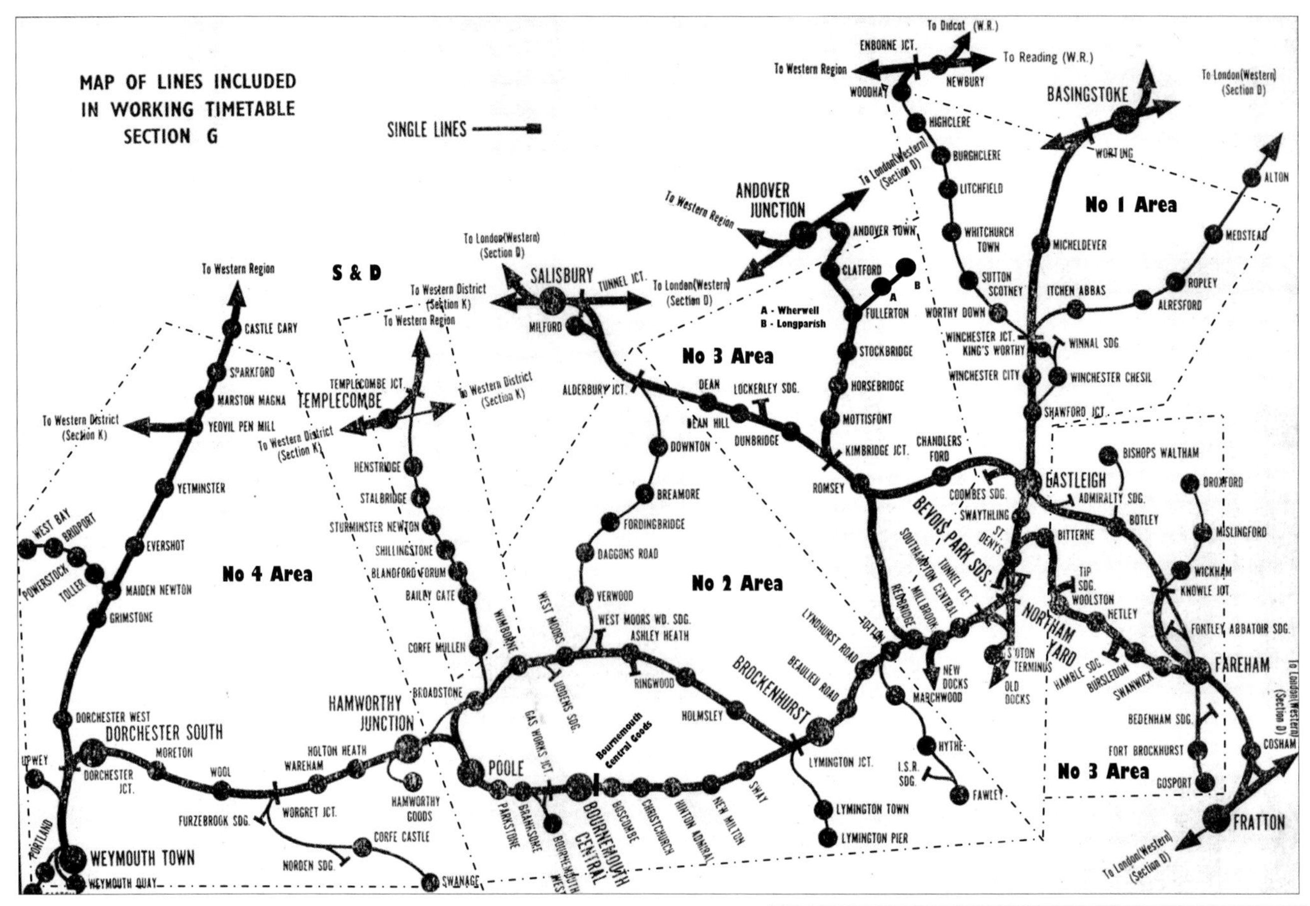


***Below*** *- Views of the Control Office are rare and this is only the second ever found. (One was also reproduced in 'Southampton Railways' by Bert Moody.) On the left side nearest the camera is K. Stephens, R. Cale, P. Andrews, H. Smith and R. White. Right hand desk nearest the camera, unknown, then Guard's Inspector E. Newham, A 'Bing' Crossley. The man at the rear on the right hand side is believed to be Mr Parker. The scene is inside the wartime office the location of which is referred to in the top view on page 28.*

***Above*** *- The District Office at Southampton, located on the up side forecourt. It was provided in 1913 and remained in use until demolished in 1971. Just visible on the right hand side is a modern extension into which the Control Office moved from the wartime structure in 1953.*
*D S Hunt.*

the Southampton area jurisdiction, coal from the Somerset mines. The only other SR district dealing with such traffic was the South Eastern with the Kent coalfield. All in all I always took the view that the S&D still regarded itself as part of the ex-Midland Railway, continuing to lean towards everything emanating from Derby!

The Southampton office was located in a house like building at the country end of Southampton Central up side station car park, but originally the TSO was some five minutes walk away in a rather forbidding looking reinforced concrete building, known as the "dug out", with no natural light but designed to withstand wartime bombing. This was situated on the up side of the railway at the Southampton Central end of Southampton tunnel. The structure can still be seen, but testament to it's strength is demonstrated by the fact it was strong enough to support a railway building constructed in the early 1960s on top, to house a new railway telephone exchange. The TSO itself was re-housed circa 1953/4 in a purpose built second floor extension on stilts built at the rear of the main office.

Very soon after starting my railway career, in May 1950 at Netley booking office, I soon became aware from the station signalmen of the TSO's existence. Somehow or other I came to the conclusion that it knew where every train was at any given moment; how wrong that assumption turned out to be. But I decided that was where I wanted to work and this was helped in early 1951 when I was transferred to the district office to work in the commercial section. I say helped, because this was Festival of Britain year, with a tremendous amount of party travel visiting the exhibition on London's South Bank and travelling by rail, thus the need for additional office staff.

Although I was not working in any operating section, at least I had gained a foothold in the district office, which I considered to be a move in the right direction. However, it was not until January 1953 when a vacancy arose as a 'recorder', duties explained later, and I commenced training - or 'learning', as the staff rosters described it! However, hardly had I been trained when the dreaded buff envelope marked 'OHMS' (not used now) landed on the doormat of my home. This was a communication received by all young men aged 18 and informing them of their National Service call-up. I was to report to the Royal Engineers training depot at Norton Barracks, Worcester, part of which I think is now beneath the M5. So I used up my residual annual leave and on 19th February joined the 09.20 Bournemouth West-Birkenhead headed by 'King Arthur' 30782 *Sir Brian* to travel to Oxford, changing there into the 11.45 Paddington-Hereford hauled by 'Castle' 7007 *Great Western*. Then after training at Merebrook Camp on the outskirts of Great Malvern and the Movements Control School, Longmoor, in August 1953 I was posted to HQ Western Command, Chester. But I am digressing too much onto the territory of "Getting Some In" – another story. Demob day came on 17th February 1955 when I gleefully joined the 12.45 Bangor-Euston at Chester with 'Jubilee' 45736 *Phoenix* in charge, crossing London to Waterloo to board the 19.30 Waterloo-Bournemouth West behind 'Battle of Britain' 34109 *Sir Trafford Leigh-Mallory* back to Southampton.

Following demob leave, I fully expected to be able to return to the TSO immediately, as there always seemed to be vacancies there. But alas, vacancies there were none and it was not until September 1955 when I returned as a recorder and also began learning the duties of a full panel clerk. When the Castle Cary-Weymouth line and Bridport branch were transferred from Western to Southern Region jurisdiction in 1958 I became one of the three panel clerks on a newly created 'Area 4', but this all came to an end on 3lst December 1962 of which more later.

As our tools of the trade, each member of staff had their own copy of the annual passenger and freight WTTs, which originally contained a vast amount of invaluable information. The Passenger WTTs contained the following lists;- symbols indicating system of working on single lines e.g. Electric Tablet, block post, One engine in steam or two or more engines coupled together etc. Instructions for compilation of guard's journals and to whom they should be sent, instructions regarding conveyance of Horse, Carriage traffic etc, working of Mixed trains and Restrictions as to the running of certain engines over portions of line. Arrival and departure times of every train was shown at every station even if station time was only half a minute. The SR was very punctilious. Freight WTTs also included single line symbols, engine restrictions and instructions as to the rendering of guard's journals. Also maximum loads for classes of engines, livestock conveyance, train formations and arrangements for supplying coal and stores to intermediate signal boxes etc.

During my period of enforced absence from the railway this format had, by 1955, vastly changed. Whilst both WTTs continued to include the system of working on single lines, the passenger TT included other lists and the freight TT only had instructions for marshalling of certain trains. By that time a separate publication was also produced for engine restrictions over the whole region.

Although WTTs operated for a year from the summer, there was a monthly supplement and at commencement of the winter TT an 'additions and alterations', known by the abbreviated term 'adds and alts'. This in itself was usually a bumper publication. It was SR practice to time light engine movements and to cater for this, there was a separate publication of pathways for such movements in the Eastleigh - Southampton and Bournemouth Central - Bournemouth West areas. The

***Opposite:*** *No doubt the best illustration of the location and working conditions for the Control staff was in 'Southampton's Railway', by Bert Moody. Originally published by Waterfront Publications in 1992 and subsequently reprinted by Atlantic.*

*On occasions the LMR would provide a locomotive type for returning empty tank cars which were deemed unsuitable for the return with a loaded train. One such occasion was on 4th March 1962, when 46141 'The North Staffordshire Regiment' appeared. It is being returned to the LMR with the 1550 Southampton (Eastern Docks) - Llandilo Jct. banana train. Where did it touch the LMR?* *(Unless stated, all photographs by the Author)*

S&D maintained its independence by producing a combined passenger and freight WTT, which also included hours of signal box opening and was similarly produced by a local printer located in Bath.

Passenger rolling stock formations were catered for in two publications. That was the Carriage Working Notice, detailing formations of all trains with a separate publication for Hampshire DEMUs. The second was an Appendix listing carriage numbers and type, e.g. BSK, FO etc, for each set and also 'loose' vehicles, the latter those not being included in a particular set. It will be recalled that the Southern was unique in keeping passenger rolling stock in neat and tidy order, by forming into numbered sets and 'loose' vehicles. EMUs and DEMUs were recognised by unit numbers. Finally there was the Rule Book, General and Sectional appendices and any other publication dealing with the railway's running.

**Organisation.**

Insofar as the TSO was concerned, the district was divided into three areas. Area 1 was, I suppose, the 'premier' of the three extending from Worting Junction to Redbridge including the Mid Hants line and DN&SR, it thus included the important Eastleigh yards and Southampton Docks. Area 2 continued westwards from Area 1 at Redbridge to Weymouth including the 'Old Road' from Brockenhurst to Poole and Hamworthy Jct. via Ringwood, the Fordingbridge line from Alderbury Jct. to West Moors together with the Fawley, Lymington, Hamworthy Goods and Swanage branches. Area 3 was cross country, from Salisbury Milford Goods to Cosham, Portcreek Jct. / Farlington Jct., the Meon Valley line, Andover Jct. via Clatford to Romsey, Gosport branch and Longparish and Bishops Waltham freight branches. The Dorchester Jct.-Weymouth section of Area 2 was, as far as SR trains were concerned, treated as a penetrating line into the WR. From history it is well known that the L&SWR had aspirations to extend westwards from Dorchester but this did not come about. A legacy of those dreams did, however, remain in that at Dorchester South up platform upon which the principal station buildings were located, faced

*Push-pull working was not the norm on the Fordingbridge line, as depicted here with Standard Class 4, 76017 arriving at Fordingbridge with the 1720 Salisbury - Bournemouth West, 28th March 1964.*

westwards. Thus up trains from Weymouth had to run past the platform and reverse back into the platform. This reverse movement was achieved in a very slick manner gained by years of experience on the part of signalmen and train crews. So instead of heading westwards, the L&SWR made do by turning south and running over the GWR line from Dorchester Jct. to Weymouth. A freight exchange point between SR and WR existed at Cemetery sidings, Dorchester Jct. duly timed in the freight WTT. This was for odd wagon loads, not complete trains. Although the SR did have a say on what went on at Weymouth, any delays to SR trains over that section of line were quickly attributed to WR causes and regulation which covered a multitude of sins. By the time I started in the TSO passenger services between Weymouth, (Melcombe Regis), Portland and Easton had already been withdrawn, but until the demise of freight, such trains were worked by Weymouth shed. The SR's MPD being at Dorchester South whilst the WR's was at Weymouth.

Under nationalisation it was logical that two such depots, separated by only a few miles, should be merged and Dorchester South was scheduled for closure. Amalgamation was not, however, achieved painlessly, as at first Weymouth WR crews were unhappy about SR crews being absorbed into their links. Nevertheless, Dorchester South lost its own locomotive allocation in March 1955. After that time engines only stabled there overnight or between duties. The shed finally closed in June 1957. Overall responsibility for the line into Weymouth changed further in 1958 when the WR line from Castle Cary to Weymouth together with the Bridport branch and freight only section from Bridport toWest Bay, Upwey Jct.- Upwey, truncated remains of the Abbotsbury branch and Portland branches were transferred to the SR. To cater for this change in the TSO, Area 2 no longer covered the main line beyond Poole and the Swanage branch. That section, plus the transferred lines from the WR thus formed a new Area 4. Three temporary clerical positions were created to cover the new area and, after experience, the positions became permanent. I was fortunate enough to be promoted into one of these new positions.

Prior to the time the SR assumed full control, we three newly appointed clerks approached the hierarchy for release from normal duties to travel over the line to 'learn the road'. Permission to do this was denied on the grounds that overtime by other staff to cover our duties was unaffordable, but we could travel over the line in our own time and to do so, would be granted use of an office free pass. Our shifts largely prevented this and about all we could do was to travel to Dorchester South after early turn, cross to Dorchester West, north to Maiden Newton and there cross onto the Bridport branch. Some staff in our new area had clearly started their railway career before nationalisation on 'God's Wonderful Railway' and in retrospect, I consider it a fair assessment to say that initially they resented being transferred to the SR. So, it was a case of attempting to understand their attitude and not insist that the Southern is always best. Likewise to display an attitude of friendliness and not antagonism. After all, we all worked to the same BR rule book. In the end, I think we all got on together.

Another function of the TSO was that of answering public train enquiries during the night hours, a scheme strenuously opposed by TSO staff when mooted by management. The then Southampton Central enquiry office dealt with both personal callers and telephone enquiries, but closed between 22.00 and 07.00. Indeed, the only purely telephone enquiry office on the SR in those days was the long established one at Waterloo. The reason TSO staff were against the scheme was because the office only had regional timetables (remember those days, one for each region?) and also no fares details. Furthermore, it was argued that, with fewer staff on duty at night, if all were engaged on train running matters, especially if services were dislocated, no staff would be would be available to deal with such enquiries. Management's response was that notwithstanding fewer staff being on duty, there was still capacity to answer calls, and times of service dislocation were rare. So a separate phone was installed normally 'dead', but switched over to the GPO network, as it was then, when the enquiry office was closed by its staff. Similarly, it was switched back to them upon reopening the following morning.

Not surprisingly TSO staff were not very enthusiastic in answering these calls but one occasion remains in my mind. The DCC's late turn finished at 22.00 and one DCC living at Eastleigh had to wait until about 22.30 for a train home. So at 22.00 he would hand over to his relief and being something of a workaholic, would occupy the wait by sitting at an empty panel and rummaging through guard's rosters or some other operating publication. One evening the enquiry 'phone rang and being a rather gruff person he simply answered: 'Yes'. I then recall him saying in similar fashion: '12.37 from the Central or 1.10 from the Terminus', which was quickly followed by: 'You asked for the first train in the morning to London and that's what I gave you'. He had quoted the times of the 'Up Mail' whilst the caller had obviously requested the time of the first train from Southampton to London in the morning, but did not mean

*Passenger services to Bishops Waltham had ceased in 1933 although freight continued until 1962. The branch also possessed its own dedicated brake-van, recorded at Botley on 18th December1961. On the same day, Class 2, No 41329 had been in charge of the freight service.*

at that early hour. No 'charm schools' or customer care courses in those days. Even if there had been it would have been doubtful if TSO staff would have been released to attend, management taking the view that overtime rates to provide cover were too costly.

Staff in the control office were purely in clerical grades, with the exception of Guards Inspectors who had worked their way up from Guards. The most senior position was that of the Chief Trains Clerk and Chief Controller, who's role was two-fold, firstly, being responsible for all matters appertaining to passenger and freight trains and secondly, supervision of current train running. His office was within the control office but was fully glass partioned all round to enable him to observe what was happening. Whilst his was nominally an 9-5 job, he positioned himself in the control on summer Saturdays, late turn on bank holiday Mondays and when any particular special train, such as a 'Royal', ran. Areas were staffed as follows;- No 1 area - three panel clerks, three recorders. No 2 area - four panel clerks, two recorders (reduced to one circa 1957), No 3 area - two panel clerks, two recorders but the latter positions were eliminated whilst I was on National service, No 4 area - three panel clerks. Having been a recorder and gained promotion to No 4 area, I was not disappointed by not having to work nights. There were originally two Guards inspectors, but they were augmented to three when the Hampshire diesel scheme commenced. Rosters were complex and we did not work the same number of hours each week, instead it was an early form of flexible rostering, which balanced over about a four week period. Some turns also involved working on two areas or the motive power panel during a single turn of duty.

Sunday working was in addition to normal weekday turns, but we were not required on duty every Sunday as with fewer trains running, fewer staff were required. Nevertheless, summer Sundays could be quite busy and I recall one Whit Sunday, this was in the days when Whit Sunday and the bank holiday Monday were on the same weekend, when the weather was fine and warm and several short notice relief trains ran down the S&D to Bournemouth and from the Bristol area to Weymouth, plus a heavy programme of Channel Island tomato trains. Quite a busy early turn.

In those days I was unmarried and so, being single, quite a proportion of my Sunday pay was donated to the Chancellor of the Exchequer. So from time to time I gave Sundays away to other staff, an offer eagerly taken up. This meant I was quite often asked by colleagues with young families and mortgages whether I wanted to work my Sunday.

The motive power panel was manned 24 hours daily, with regular staff on it having their own set of permanent engine diagrams and also, on the panel, a regional locomotive allocation list, all frequently perused by me. Both permanent and special engine diagrams, the latter to cover bank holidays, boat trains and other special

| DOWN | Start | C Cary | † | * | Mins. late arr. |
|---|---|---|---|---|---|
| 8.31 Warehm—Swnge | | — | — | — | |
| 8.30 Bmth W—Warehm (8.28 S.O. to 9/9) | — | — | — | — | |
| 6. 0 Cdiff—Weymth S.O. 1/7 to 26/8 | — | | | | |
| 9v16 Yl PM—Yl Tn | ☐ | — | — | — | — |
| 9.28 M Ntn—Weymth (9.32 S.O. to 9/9) | | — | — | — | |
| 5.40 Wloo—Weymth | — | — | | | |
| 7v25 Wbury—Weymth | — | ☐ | ☐ | ☐ | ☐ |
| 9.56 Yl PM—Tauntn (9.54 S.O. to 9/9) | | — | — | — | — |
| 9.42 Warehm—Swnge | | — | — | — | |
| 8. 5 Brstl—Weymth | — | | | | |
| 10. 5 Yl PM—Weymth S.X. (24/7 to 25/8) | | — | — | | |
| 10.36 Brid—M Ntn (10.34 S.O.) To 9/9 | | — | — | — | |
| 8.50 Salis—Swnge S.X. (24/7 to 25/8) | — | — | | — | |
| 11. 4 / 11. 0 Brid—M Ntn frm 11/9 S.O. to 9/9 | | — | — | — | |
| 7.20 Wloo—Weymouth S.O. 24/6 to 19/8 | — | — | | | |
| 9. 5 Salis—Weymth S.X. (17/7 to 1/9) | — | — | | | |
| 10.25 Warehm—Swnge S.X. to 9/9 | | — | — | — | |
| Total: Trains | | | | | |
| Minutes | | | | | |

| UP | Start |
|---|---|
| 9.20 Swnge—Warehm (9.15 to Wloo S.O. to 9/9) | |
| 9.17 Weymth—Wloo (9.20 S.O. to 9/9) | |
| 9.25 Weymth—Bghm S.O. 29/7 to 26/8 | |
| 9.35 Weymth—Yl PM (Yl Tn S.O. to 9/9) | |
| 10. 0 Weymth—Whmptn S.O. 24/6 to 9/9 | |
| 10.12 M Ntn—Brid | |
| 10.30 Swnge—Warehm To 9/9 (10.13 S.O.) | |
| 10.10 Weymth—Bmth C (To Wloo S.O. to 9/9) | |
| 9.45 Tauntn—Yl PM (10.5 S.O. to 9/9) | — |
| 10.20 S.O. Weymth—Whmptn To 9/9 | |
| 11.27 M Ntn—Brid (11.15 S.X. to 9/9) (11.25 S.O. to 9/9) | |
| 10.37 Weymth—Yl PM S.O. to 9/9 | |
| 10.50 Swnge—Warehm (S.X. to 9/9) 11.10 to 8/9 | |
| 11.28 Yl Tn—Yl PM | — |
| 11. 5 Weymth—Brstl (11.12 to Padd S.O. to 9/9) | |
| 11. 2 Weymth } Wloo S.O. to 9/9 | |
| 11.34 Swnge } Wloo S.O. to 9/9 | |
| Total: Trains | |
| Minutes | |

† Yl PM or Wareham.
* M Nton or Dor S.

*An extract of one of the passenger train running sheets referred on page 40, this one for No 4 area. Sheets were prepared for a whole year, so included summer only trains and other such variations, van trains being indicated by a thickened black square. The first column was the starting time for trains starting in the area, e.g. 8.31 Wareham - Swanage. The second column being the "in district" time at Castle Cary (reported by Sparkford box or Yeovil Pen Mill when Sparkford was switched out). The third column is time at Wareham (for trains from the Bournemouth direction) and Yeovil Pen Mill (for trains from the Castle Cary direction), followed in the forth column by times at Dorchester South or Maiden Newton for trains from the Bournemouth or Castle Cary direction respectively. The final column, was destination station arrival time for trains terminating in the area, which was all trains in the down direction. Delay explanations were written in the lined space in the middle, down trains on the left and ups on the right.*

traffic requirements, were compiled at Waterloo. These special rosters arrived at Southampton Mondays to Fridays and Saturdays on the 21.30 and 15.20 Waterloo respectively, with the panel clerk collecting them from the Central station. Part of the night clerk's duty was to thoroughly scrutinise the special rosters to ensure every movement in special traffic notices was covered. In the rare event of any not being covered, he had to arrange coverage with motive power depots and any other control concerned. Liaison had also to be maintained with MPDs to balance locomotives. For instance, if a Nine Elms loco had been stopped upon arrival at Bournemouth, when repairs were complete he had to arrange for it to be worked back to Nine Elms. A 24 hour MP log was maintained of times of all messages regarding MP matters and details and time of action taken. A copy of this was sent to Eastleigh MPD every morning at about 08.00 for perusal by the District Motive Power Superintendent.

Permanent guards' rosters were compiled by district staff departments, there being no such term as 'human resources' in those days. Therefore the control guards inspectors dealt with day to day short notice alterations and also covered special traffic working. At that time there was a large guards roster section at Waterloo which dealt with London West District matters, liaising with other districts as necessary. I always felt roster compilation was an art and clerks working in these sections, often with years of experience, were certainly masters of their craft often knowing many rosters off by heart, together with the contents of national industrial agreements. I do wonder whether such experience exists today.

43

82014
ST DENYS

The other remaining work in the Control to be described is that of 'Through Vehicles' although the other regions referred to this as 'tail traffic. Through vehicles were actually part of the Special Traffic section, but for ease of contact with stations etc, it was done in the Control whose staff had to deal with it at night and on Sundays. The work consisted of arranging services for movement of non-regular, passenger rated van traffic, not shown in carriage working notices. In other words, it was of an occasional nature and consisted of such traffic as horse boxes, corpses (carried in a separate van always attached to a passenger working), vans of overseas mail for specific ocean liners and especially in summer, vans of theatrical scenery for touring theatrical companies performing in seaside resorts.

A trap for new Control and Through Vehicles staff was having knowledge of the non-written instructions prohibiting the attachment of vans etc to certain trains.

***Opposite top*** *- Following the introduction of the 18 Hampshire DEMUs to local services in the south of the county during September and November 1957, two problems quickly arose. The first was scheduling time for adequate maintenance and the second, that the original two-car sets quickly became overcrowded. For a while it was not unusual to witness what would not be regarded as some strange combinations and workings, including the combination of three 2-car units, Nos 1102, 1113 and 1103, photographed between Netley and Sholing on the 1638 Portsmouth & Southsea to Southampton Central service, 15th April 1959. The reason was an evening football match at Fratton Park, Portsmouth which meant that the return train for Southampton would be heavily loaded.*

***Opposite bottom*** *- To allow for increased maintenance times, some trains on the Andover Junction / Eastleigh / Portsmouth axis returned for a while to steam traction with extended schedules. One such was the 1445 Andover Junction - Southampton Terminus, with Class 2 No 82014 at St Denys on 8th May 1959.*

***Above*** *- The difficulties with overcrowding on the diesel sets during peak periods and during the summer, necessitated 'steam relief' services. One of these was the 1732 Portsmouth & Southsea to Southampton Central, having just passed Sholing behind 'L1' No 31753 on 9th August 1959.*

*'7F' 2-8-0 No 53809 passes Parkstone on the 0908 (SO) Birmingham New Street - Bournemouth West. 18th August 1962. These locomotives were not often seen south of Templecombe in the winter, being more often employed in those months to attack the Mendip gradients on freight trains. The heaviest passenger train on the S & D in the winter was the 'Pines Express', which was easily handled by Std. Cl5 4-6-0s with, of course, an assisting engine between Evercreech Jct. and Bath. Summer Saturdays, however, presented a different situation with heavy trains to Bournemouth West conveying eager passengers from the Midlands and North of England to their annual seaside holiday and returning them home. It was on these trains that the 2-8-0s found themselves on such summer Saturdays.*

Two such instructions readily come to mind. The first concerned the 06.50 Reading General -Southampton Terminus and 08.00 Romsey - Weymouth. To interconnect at Eastleigh the Reading train was booked there at 08.21 - 08.28 and the Romsey train at 08.15 - 08.35. Both trains could be considered as 'mini-commuter', as the Reading train conveyed employees working in the numerous shipping offices, then located in close proximity to Southampton Terminus station, whilst the Romsey train conveyed those working in offices and shops in the central area of Southampton and also the railway hierarchy of the district office. The other instruction related to the 14.20 Weymouth - Andover Jct. via Eastleigh and Romsey. This was a curious train, meandering its way across Dorset and Hampshire calling at all stations except Swaythling. So why then not call at Swaythling? Simply because the booked arrival time at Eastleigh was 17.22, just three minutes after the up 'Bournemouth Belle' had left Southampton Central, so if a van had been attached somewhere en-route and the service lost time, the 'Belle' may have sighted a distant signal 'on'. Such a delay to the 'Belle' would be severely frowned upon!

Returning to the morning workings; one Through Vehicles clerk, new to the job, had not been informed of the ban on transferring vehicles between the Reading - Southampton Terminus and Romsey-Weymouth trains at Eastleigh. The Reading train was also particularly handy, being useful to convey vans for Bournemouth and Weymouth etc which had arrived at Reading overnight. This arrangement was, in fact, already catered for, as upon arrival at Southampton Terminus, the stock of the Reading train formed a stopper for Bournemouth, thus there was no need for vans to be transferred at Eastleigh. This clerk, however, decided that an earlier arrival at Bournemouth could be effected by transferring a van one day at Eastleigh. Unfortunately all did not go well at Eastleigh and both trains were delayed. Needless to say he was hauled up before a superior and given 'suitable advice' for the future.

**Details of Train Running.**

I don't know about other regions but the Southern seemed to be obsessed with statistics. As a Recorder the night turn commenced at 23.00 and most certainly around the first two hours were occupied by compiling statistics for the 24 hour period midnight to midnight. For instance, at every station where trains reached the end of their journey, the number of trains terminating was totalled and an average number of minutes late arrival was struck from the total number of minutes arriving late. So for stations with a fair number, such as Bournemouth West to those with one solitary terminating train, such as Bitterne, this was a test of one's mathematical skills. All statistical details had to be telephoned to HQ Control, Waterloo. Then there were what was known as 'selecteds', generally consisting of departures from Waterloo at 30 minutes past the hour and the corresponding up services of principal trains to Bournemouth and Weymouth plus a few slower services. Also included were cross country services on the Portsmouth to Bristol - Cardiff axis but nothing on the S&D. Surprisingly even 'The Pines Express' was not included until re-routed via Basingstoke and Oxford in 1962. Some van and all fish trains were included and main freight services from and to Nine Elms and Feltham.

*Saturday 29th June 1957 was not a good day for the motive power department with engine failures on up morning services. The first resulted in 'Q' class 0-6-0 No 30548 being purloined to work the 0932 (SO) Bournemouth - Central to Wolverhampton, seen passing St Denys at 1045. The service was already running about 10 minutes late at this point. Shortly afterwards another failure resulted in 'Q1' No 33005 at the head of the 1050 (SO) Hinton Admiral to Waterloo, this time recorded at St Denys at 1200 and some 30 minutes behind time. The identity of and circumstances surrounding the failures of the booked locomotives for these services is unknown. The lines coming in from the left are from Fareham via Netley.*

Progress of these trains had to be given to Waterloo at fairly frequent intervals throughout the day. Also reported to Waterloo were passenger loadings and the timekeeping of all Southampton ocean liner boat trains and similar services for cross-channel boats and of course the 'Bournemouth Belle'.

These statistics and details were generally haggled over by the daily morning passenger conference held between officers in the Chief Operating Manager's department at Waterloo and all districts. There was a similar freight conference but I always felt this was more business-like, as it dealt with orders and numbers of empty wagons returning to other regions for coal etc. Meanwhile, in the reverse direction, track was kept on the number of banana vans worked to Southampton Docks when a banana boat was due, and after the SR take-over of the Castle Cary-Weymouth line, whether sufficient empty vanfits were available at Weymouth in the season for Channel Island tomato traffic.

It was the duty of certain signalboxes, especially those on the extremity of the district boundary, to report train passing times. This was often done in groups. Any delay of five minutes or more anywhere was supposed to be reported promptly, but this was not always done and we quite often had to, 'search' for delays. Passenger trains were recorded as 'minutes late', with red digits denoting early or 'before time' running on large sheets of paper. Each area had its individual set of sheets listing every train running in the area. As quite a number of trains ran in summer only, it followed that a considerable number of columns were unused outside the summer timetable. Sheets were prepared and printed annually to coincide with issues of the WTT. It was the recorders job to obtain the times from the signal boxes and amend the 'master copy' sheet each time a timetable supplement was issued. One set of sheets per 24 hours was used, running from midnight to midnight. It follows that, if train times were not reported currently, there was no way the location of any train was known, so shattering my opinion referred to earlier! Empty trains were not included on sheets, as they were not included in statistics, but a watchful eye was kept on these as well.

Freight trains were recorded on separate sheets but not necessarily by the same signal boxes as passenger trains were. For freight, only starting and terminating times were shown and then as minutes late, actual times being recorded as intermediate passing times.

**Service Disruption.**

When services were sufficiently late to upset train crew rosters, the TSO had to take measures to reduce late running of the crew's next part of the roster. Whilst signalmen often made their own regulation decisions, from time to time they would ask the TSO for a decision as to which train should be given preference. Furthermore, knowing that a train or trains were running late, the TSO would consult with signalmen and give direction before advice was sought. This was no reflection on signalmen, but it needs to be remembered that today's large panel

***Opposite page*** - *With no turntable at Fawley and several ungated level crossings, operating wise the Fawley branch was a problem, especially when tank car loads increased from the late 1950s onwards. Sharing the duties at this time were the 'H16', 'Ivatt Class 2 and 'BR' Standard variant of the latter. No 82012 is passing Southampton Central at 1440 with 1412 Eastleigh east yard - Fawley freight, on 14th February 1960.*

***Above*** - *Bigger motive power was required once on the main line, which often produced unusual sights - for the South Western main line at least. '8F' No 48230 casts a smoke screen over St Denys five minutes after getting to grips with the 2000 (SO) Bevois Park - Spondon, routed via the DNS line, on a very dull 30th July 1960. On the extreme right, the van is standing on the short Crawford's Biscuits private siding.*

*Larger still, '9F' No 92150 passing Southampton Central at 1150 on the heavy 1025 Fawley - Bromford Bridge, via the DNS line. The engine had taken over this train at Millbrook yard, tender locomotives not being permitted on the Fawley branch. Other full trains might see the engine change take place at Totton or Eastleigh. Four members of the class were transferred to Eastleigh especially for these workings, until haulage was given over to D65xx diesels. 18th April 1962.*

boxes were unknown and, at larger stations, more than one box controlled a station area. For instance, Eastleigh station and yards required four boxes, Allbrook, Eastleigh East, Eastleigh West and on the Portsmouth line, Eastleigh South, to control the area, plus ground frames in the East and marshalling yards. Therefore signalmen could really only regulate traffic as it affected their patch, so different from today's modern panel boxes which can oversee and plan movements over a wide area.

Summer Saturdays and bank holiday Monday evenings were particular times when careful regulation was required on the Bournemouth main line to fit in stopping trains when faster services were running late. For instance, in the down direction, after leaving Southampton Central there were only two places, Brockenhurst and Pokesdown, where stopping trains could be looped before reaching Bournemouth Central. But even then, by looping at Brockenhurst, delay could be caused to Lymington branch or 'Old Road' trains. In those days any suggestion that engineering work should completely close a section of line during a bank holiday weekend, especially on a Monday, would have been received with derision.

If the first train in the up Summer Saturday morning procession lost time due to its engine, several of us would pin the cause to the fact that it was probably hauled by a Urie 'King Arthur'. But perhaps this was unfair criticism of these locomotives, as they were still doing stirling work. Late Saturday afternoons could be tricky when trains from the north of England, via both Oxford and the S&D bound for Bournemouth, usually presented themselves late. Services from the Midlands via Oxford to Portsmouth and Bournemouth generally arrived after mid-day.

Some summer Saturday trains started from smaller stations, not principal coastal resorts, so as to give passengers joining at other stations a chance to obtain a seat. Such trains that come to mind are the 08.47 Pokesdown – Birkenhead (stock empty from Bournemouth Central Goods having been berthed there all week), 08.48 New Milton - Swansea via Fordingbridge (stock empty from Brockenhurst yard) and 10.50 Hinton Admiral - Waterloo (stock empty from Hamworthy Jct the previous evening and berthed in the up side long siding at the Bournemouth end of the station).

Bank holiday weekends could create problems of their own, depending upon the weather. The special traffic 'P' notices and stencil notices contained timings and stock workings of excursion trains, some originating on other regions, to such seaside resorts as Portsmouth, Bournemouth, Swanage and Weymouth. Also ordinary services were strengthened with additional coaches. Return trains and strengthenings were made from late afternoon, early evening onwards and such arrangements were usually adequate, providing the weather was fine. Wet weather in the morning naturally inhibited people from venturing out, but if the day dawned sunny and warm, but deteriorated during the afternoon, there was trouble! Those travelling by special excursion trains had to wait until the advertised time of such trains whereas ordinary service users started their homeward journey during the afternoon cramming themselves into un-strengthened trains, unless it was possible to provide additional stock at short notice. We tried to do this wherever practicable but were not always successful. On some summer Sundays, excursion trains were included in the WTT, which on some Sundays opened such lines as the DN&SR, normally closed on the Lord's day.

**'Pinch Points'**

Unlike many seaside resorts on other Regions, none in the Southampton district had excursion platforms, thus places such as Bournemouth and Weymouth had no spare bolt holes. In the Bournemouth area, Bournemouth Central had only two carriage sidings which were quite a distance from the station, although it did have one through road in each direction passing through the station, where some stock was berthed from time to time.

Bournemouth West had carriage sidings, but these could not accommodate all the additional summer workings, so stock was worked out to such places as Hamworthy Jct, Wimborne and Bournemouth Central Goods, where it was still expected for trains to be cleaned and watered. Weymouth was also cramped, but after the SR took over, siding accommodation was expanded.

**Train Cancellations**

Except when major disruption occurred, passenger train cancellations were virtually unknown in the Southampton district. If for example a passenger guard was short, then a goods guard was usually substituted. Passenger guards did not work freight trains, but goods guards could work passenger trains. However, the coming of the Hampshire DEMUs did see some cancellations especially following a unit failure. This would be until a replacement could be obtained and slotted into the circuit working of the failed train. Freight train cancellations did crop up from time to time, when there was no traffic for a particular service, e.g a timetabled empty wagon train returning such wagons to a particular destination.

**Signal Boxes**

It is important to remember that today's familiar large panel boxes had yet to become a twinkle in the eye of signal engineers. Colour light signalling (CLS), except in London termini areas, was generally in its infancy so far as the Southampton district was concerned, being confined principally to intermediate signals - especially on the main line north of Winchester. So mechanical boxes predominated and a few were only open on 'high days and holidays' (summer Saturdays , late turn bank holiday Mondays and to meet special traffic demands). When on nights, one had to remember which boxes were open 24/7, such knowledge being acquired in time. Boxes not open for 24 hours seemed to open and close at different times morning and evening respectively. Then, of course, not all boxes were open on Sundays!

**Locomotive Workings**

Southern Region locomotives working in the district over the years have been well chronicled and photographed, so I will only comment on the more unusual, of these I suppose the three Brighton duties came into this category.

The first of these was the 09.40 Brighton - Bournemouth West, returning at 13.50 and as far as Salisbury the 11.00 Brighton-Cardiff returning on the 11.00 Plymouth Friary - Brighton and 11.30 Brighton - Plymouth Friary, returning on the 13.00 Cardiff - Brighton. The Plymouth and Cardiff trains conveyed Portsmouth portions, attached on the outward journey at Fareham and detached there in the opposite direction but Portsmouth had separate trains on summer Saturdays. Sundays saw an out and back Brighton - Bournemouth West, but in the summers of 1958 - 1962 inclusive, the Brighton - Plymouth Friary ran. For these duties, Brighton had an allocation of West Country pacifics, but use of the handsome Marsh Atlantics was by no means unknown on the Bournemouth turn, especially in summer. From time to time Standard Class 4 2-6-4Ts, U1 moguls and Schools were also used.

From the 1961 summer timetable, the return Bournemouth West - Brighton train was retimed to start at 18.35. One explanation I came across for this but which cannot be guaranteed as authentic was that it was an attempt to attract holidaymakers staying at Sussex coast resorts onto a day trip to the Bournemouth area. If that was correct, by the time such passengers returned to their hotels they would have missed their evening meal. The change of time for the return train really meant rosters for the footplate crew and probably the guard as well, became uneconomic. Whereas with the original timing it was an 'out and home' working, it was not so with the new evening return time, when Bournemouth men worked to Southampton Central where they were relieved by Brighton men who had traveled over 'on the cushions'. One day, the outward train had reached Bournemouth without hindrance, but in the course of the day an EMU was derailed, I think at Ford in Sussex, blocking both lines. I was on the turn finishing at 17.30, the latter part of which was on the MP panel and thought nothing about the return train having received no approach from either the area panel or Central Division TSO at Redhill. The train duly arrived at Southampton Central where there was no Brighton crew to relieve the Bournemouth men. As Bournemouth men bad no road knowledge of the Netley line, there was no alternative but to terminate the train. The following day I was hauled over the coals by the CTC for not checking with Redhill as to whether the Brighton men would reach Southampton. This incident illustrates the fact that we did not get things right all of the time but whilst I recall my own involvement, I have no recollection of how the Plymouth and Cardiff - Brighton through trains fared, which left our patch in the late afternoon. How the human mind works.

On summer Saturdays through trains ran from Waterloo to both Lymington Pier and Swanage. Engines on Swanage trains either changed at Wareham or ran through to Swanage. Furthermore, most of these latter trains were routed via the 'Old Road', also known as 'Castleman's Corkscrew', after the promoter and sinuous nature of the line and the Broadstone - Hamworthy Jct. single line which was traversed by few passenger trains.

Lymington Pier trains, however, changed engines at Brockenhurst where a short length turntable was located, so restricting the size of locomotives working from Waterloo. To work these trains some U1 2-6-0s from the Eastern Section were transferred for the summer to Nine Elms, but upon arrival of new Standard Class 4 2-6-0s at Eastleigh, which in turn displaced the large Drummond D15 4-4-0s there, the D15s were surprisingly transferred to Nine Elms for the Lymington Pier trains. In turn, they were replaced by Schools displaced from the Eastern Section by Hastings DEMUs and Kent Coast electrification. When the Class 33s came along, they took charge of both Lymington Pier and Swanage trains working them throughout.

***A further instalment of this fascinating account will appear shortly.***

*The Harbour Board lines provided a connection between Southampton New and Old Docks, (now the Western and Eastern Docks respectively), often running alongside and across public streets and also serving the Town Quay.*
***Opposite page*** - *'USA' No 30072 is crossing over the Royal Pier approach road on a west to east transfer trip. 2nd August 1962.*
***This page, top*** - *Diminutive 'C14' 0-4-0T, No 77s, still designated as working for the Engineer's department at Redbridge, but displaced from this duty by a 'USA' tank. It is seen shunting Town Quay sidings.10th January 1959.*
***Below*** - *Following cosmetic attention at Eastleigh Works, 'T3' 4-4-0 No 563 sets off for preservation at Clapham Museum by road transport. It is being loaded from sidings that now form part of the Red Funnel car-park, 25th January 1961. (The restoration of No 563 and its road transfer were referred to on page 82 of 'Southern Way No 4').*

2
DMV
980

# EVERY PICTURE TELLS A STORY…

## *"On Manoeuvres by the Meon Valley line"*

**Christopher Purdie**

This intriguing photograph recently came to light by pure chance in a box of old War Office photos at a military bookseller's stand at the Bovington Tank Museum.

The location was instantly recognisable from a photograph in Ray Stone's *MEON VALLEY RAILWAY* as the Hedge Corner road junction on the A32 Alton to Fareham road between East Tisted and Privett, this despite the fact that the bridge has long been demolished. Similarly the adjacent embankments have also been levelled although a clue as to the location can still be gained in the 21st century by the presence of a lay-by either side of the present day junction and which was once the course of the original A32 prior to being straightened. As depicted here, the main A32 runs left to right under the bridge, with the Alton direction to the right. The junction was in effect a staggered crossroads at this point and in the immediate foreground part of the Petersfield road. Opposite the road leading towards Monkwood and Ropley can be seen.

*- Continued overleaf*

Just out of sight on the right hand side of the bridge at the top of the embankment, was an open fronted timber lean-to shelter, used by the permanent-way department to store a motorised trolley.

The photo bears the caption 'Mechanised Cavalry' and is a wonderful study of different elements of a mechanised cavalry unit on exercise shortly before WW2. Light tanks, tank crew, a signals truck and a despatch rider are all pictured. So who were they? The clue to the unit's identity is the regimental badge on the side of the turret of the tank in the left of the photograph. Under a magnifying glass, the shape of the badge appears to match that of the 4th Queens Own Hussars

The regimental history of the 4th Queen's Own Hussars states that the regiment was mechanised in 1936, initially trading its horses for lorries. In November 1937, less than two years before the outbreak of WW2, the regiment took delivery of its first tanks, the Vickers Mark VIB light tank, as seen in the photo. At this time, the regiment was based at Aldershot, transferring to Tidworth in October 1938 with 1st Cavalry Brigade. Given the leaves on the trees in the photo and the greater likelihood of the unit being 'on manoeuvres' from Aldershot rather than Tidworth, the photo was almost certainly taken in 1938.

A similar photograph is located on the Imperial War Museum website, although there it is described as involving the Royal Tank Corps. This cannot be correct, as the uniforms of the two were significantly different at the time. Indeed, at first glance, to non-military enthusiasts, the tank crewmen's uniforms bear a certain similarity to those of the German Panzertruppen. The thought that this might have been joint manoeuvres can be instantly discounted; had we of course been invaded, then scenes like this might have been all too familiar.

Further study led to an approach to the staff of Bovington Tank Museum, who were able to confirm the researcher's hunches as adding further detail as to the road vehicles. The truck in the foreground is a Morris-Commercial, possibly with an 'office' body, while the other one is also possibly a Morris but this time with a regular 15cwt truck body. The motorcycle, possibly a Triumph, has not been identified at this stage - perhaps a knowledgeable reader of 'SW' can help...?

*A considerable amount of previously unpublished material on the Meon Valley line has recently become available and Denis Tilman has kindly offered to annotate this in the near future.*

# 'Atlantic Moment'

*No 38, the name 'Portland Bill' was not added 1925, inside Victoria circa 1911. (Almost exactly the same location but some years later and with electric traction,, features on the cover of 'SW5'.)*

*Classified as class 'B5' when entering service in 1905, the designation was altered to 'H Atlantic' in February 1906 and finally to 'H1' in January 1907.*

*There were five members of the class, all of which passed into Southern railway ownership in 1923, with Nos 37-39 lasting into British Railway's days. They were condemned and cut up in 1951.*

*Roger Carpenter collection.*

# The SOUTHERN RAILWAY: from Inception, through to Nationalisation and beyond.

# Part 1 - The Legacy

## Tony Goodyear

This series of articles is not intended to introduce large amounts of new material into the debate, on what is already a well documented subject. The author's intention is to take a more strategic look at the documentation available from various sources. Over the years much has been written about particular aspects of the Southern story but in this series I shall look back in time, well beyond the formation of the Southern Railway and attempt to pull the various fragmented pieces of the story together, in an effort to give an insight into the way the "Southern Railway" came together and was then moulded into the very distinctive system it became, much of which still exists today, both as physical infrastructure and the services operated by today's privatised railway.

The setting up of the Southern Railway was as a result of the `Railways Act, 1921', which received the Royal Assent on August 19th of that year. This started a process to amalgamate the railway companies of Great Britain into four large groups the 'Big Four', which later became known as the "Grouping". The grouping together of the railway companies in this way was in many respects a compromise, as at the time most political commentators expected the railways to be nationalised.

In his book `A History of the Southern Railway' C F Dendy Marshall states that "The ACT spoke of five `constituent companies' in the Southern Group". First thoughts suggest that there should only be three, second thoughts, perhaps four, but five? Marshall lists the companies as: the London & South Western (L&SWR), the London Brighton & South Coast (LB&SCR), the South Eastern (SER), the London Chatham and Dover (LC&DR) and the South Eastern and Chatham Railway Companies' Managing Committee (SE&CR). Marshall goes on to say that the SE&CR should not have been included because it had no issued stock. Clearly the reason for the LC&DR and the SER being included was because, at that time they were still operating railway companies, with assets, share holders and quoted on the stock market. The reason for including the SE&CR was more likely to have been because it had assets and liabilities. By specifically naming the SE&CR in the act it ensured that assets got absorbed and liabilities discharged.

An Amalgamation Tribunal was set up to agree the proposals of the various companies for each of the four groups being formed. Their first task was to approve the financial proposals, including the issue of new stock. For the Southern Group this amounted to £144,840,215 (approximately £6 billion at 2007 prices) of capital and was issued in ten classes, including loans.

Following approval of the financial aspects, the tribunal dealt with absorption schemes put forward by both the LB&SCR and the L&SWR. With only five companies mentioned in the act, there was some tidying up to do. The LB&SCR asked for the Hayling. The Brighton and Dyke companies to be absorbed, the former was straightforward but with the latter no agreement was reached, as it was in the hands of the receiver. The L&SWR asked for the Bridgewater (BR) (Edington Junction to Bridgewater opened 21st July 1890, which was owned by the Bridgewater Railway, leased by L&SWR who in turn leased it to the Somerset & Dorset Joint Committee who worked it as part of their system.), Isle of Wight (IWR), Isle of Wight Central (IWCR), Sidmouth, North Cornwall (NCR), Plymouth and Dartmoor, Plymouth Devonport and South Western Junction Railway (PD&SWJR) to be absorbed.

Even after the amalgamation was approved by the tribunal, it was necessary to include: the Greenwich, Victoria Station, Pimlico and the Mid Kent, which were of course worked by the SE&CR committee. This still left the Lee-on-the-Solent (quite why this got left to the end is not recorded), Brighton and Dyke and the Freshwater, Yarmouth & Newport (FY&N). Dendy Marshall records that the Southern objected to the B&D's liabilities of £14,000 or more being transferred, as the company was insolvent and the debts could not be paid. The Southern argued that as receipts did not exceed £1,400 a year and the land was owned by the War Office and could be recovered at any time without compensation, it should not be required to take on the liabilities. The tribunal decided that the liabilities should be taken along with the line. The

*The exterior of the SECR portion of Victoria Station in the early 1900s.* *RHCH / Spence Collection*

case was subsequently taken to the court of appeal and it was dismissed there in July 1923. There was talk of the matter being taken to the House of Lords, but evidently the Southern thought better of it and let the matter drop. The FY&N case was a little different, as they contended that allowance should be made in the settlement for future income from the proposed Solent tunnel! It was considered a bit far fetched at the time and the tribunal refused to take it in to consideration.

Many of the Railway Companies listed above existed in little more than name only, in some cases they owned the infrastructure and received payments from the operating company, subsequently paying dividends to their shareholders after the deduction of expenses. However, in four instances they were fully functioning railways with staff and rolling stock as well as being responsible for their own maintainece. In several cases the absorption process became fraught, involving much management time in sorting out the detail. As mentioned above the FY&N was one that held out against the inevitable.

To be able to appreciate what happened after the grouping and to understand some of the priorities forced upon the new company, we have to look back well beyond the formation of Southern Railway at some of the inherited lines and their status. Starting in the West Country the apparently small PD&SWJR was set up by an act of 1883 to enable the building of a railway from Lydford to Devonport, thus enabling the L&SWR to avoid having to use the single track GWR line between Lydford and Tavistock Junction, to gain access to the L&SWR station at Devonport, which the L&SWR had been doing since May 1876. At the grouping the PD&SWJR was in a most unusual situation, in that part of the railway was leased and operated by the LSWR the other part being operated entirely by the PD&SWJR using its own locomotives and stock. This all came about because the PD&SWJR was required to purchase the 3ft. 6in. gauge East Cornwall Minerals Railway, whose directors forced a clause in a subsequent act of 1884 requiring the purchase. The PD&SWJR converted the line to standard gauge and extended it, to form a connection with the main line at Bere Alston in 1908 and instead of leasing it to the

L&SWR ended up operating it themselves. Interestingly, it produced reasonable returns for its investors.

The next part of the story takes us to the Isle of Wight and the mostly impoverished and squabbling undertakings that existed there. Although efforts had been made over the years to amalgamate the five separate railway operating entities on the Island into one company, the usual animosities between them ultimately prevented agreement and progress. Such was the state of affairs that in 1877 the L&SWR and the LB&SCR jointly took the unprecedented step of promoting a bill to build a railway pier, which would allow their steamers to berth at all states of the tide, together with a station at the Pier Head and their own railway from Ryde St Johns Road to the new station on the pier at Ryde. The new line came into use in early 1880 as far as Esplanade (the only intermediate station) and to the Pier Head in the July. I know of no other instance in Britain where a railway was built as a joint line, where neither of two owning companies ever ran a train over it and the line was used by two other separate railway companies, who had no interest in it but both benefited. Indeed the IWR even claimed £3058 in damages, for loss of business at their refreshment rooms, during construction. This was eventually settled by arbitration at £1033. Even then the IWR wrote to the joint committee a few months later, asking to rent the arches under the new road bridge for a nominal sum and suggested that the joint committee should be able to fit them up at little cost. The joint committee wrote back reminding them that they had been paid their compensation, none the less some sort of deal was done. The indignity of having two main line railway companies having to promote a bill before parliament to build their own facilities on the Island may have forced further action by the smaller companies to join forces. As by an act of 1887 the Cowes & Newport Railway (CNR) and the first line to open, the Ryde & Newport Railway (RNR) and the Isle of Wight & Newport Junction Railway (IW&NJR) were amalgamated to form the Isle of Central Railway (IWCR).

As part of the amalgamation process the L&SWR took the lead in acquiring the lines on the Isle of Wight,

*The exterior of the old LBSCR Victoria station prior to rebuilding. The large building to the right is the Grosvenor Hotel. 30th June 1904.*

*Interior of the rebuilt (LBSCR) Victoria, recorded on 19th October 1906. At this time the platforms seen were reported as open for local traffic.*

following the passing of the act the L&SWR lost no time in arranging inspections of the islands railways during the latter part of 1921. These were carried out by Sir Herbert Walker, who was also involved in the subsequent negotiations. Fairly amicable settlements were agreed with the IWR and the IWCR but as described earlier the FYN decided to contest the £50,000 offered only to have their claim turned down. The IWR chose to negotiate with the L&SWR and as a result obtained a marginally more favourable deal for their shareholders. The new order came into being on 1 January 1923 and for the first time the Isle of Wight had a unified railway system, on paper at least. It would be some years before changes and improvements worked through the system, although the L&SWR had clearly seen things they did not like and had plans well in hand to remedy some of the shortcomings by the time the new company got down to business.

We now turn to the three major constituents of the new Southern Railway by looking at the mighty London & South Western Railway first. I use the word mighty comparatively, because the L&SWR was only a medium sized company in terms of pre grouping railway companies generally but was by far the largest constituent of the Southern Group, both in terms of route mileage and financial clout. At 1019 route miles it was more than twice the size of the LB&SCR and nearly 40% bigger than the SE&CR. The other massive contribution was Southampton Docks, which the L&SWR had prudently purchased on 1 November 1892. The L&SWR had been lending the Southampton Dock Co. money for much needed improvements since a loan of £250,000 was provided in 1886, following approval by parliament. Prior to the loan the Southampton Dock Co. had been looking towards the local municipal authorities to provide financial support through a take over but, in those far off days, what effectively amounted to nationalisation was not considered an option. This shrewd decision enabled the L&SWR and later the Southern to consistently improve the docks over the fifty to sixty years up to the outbreak of World War II, in so doing generating unbelievable quantities of traffic for themselves and any one else who could get in on the act, some clearly being more welcome than others.

It should also be noted that the L&SWR was a totally ruthless organisation, with an extremely able management team. From its earliest days events had proved that it was quite capable of some very underhanded dealings, from time to time. It is most likely that it was this opportunistic and ruthless streak that fuelled the often terse relations with the Great Western, whose dealings with L&SWR were always overshadowed by a deep mistrust of their intentions. A number of these events are significant to the story and going back to the early days, the little Bodmin & Wadebridge Railway was acquired by a group of L&SWR directors in 1846, without the approval of parliament and it was to be another forty years before it was legally absorbed in to the L&SWR in 1886. In 1846 the nearest point that the L&SWR came to Bodmin or Wadebridge, was Salisbury, a good 200 miles distant. It was to be 39 years later in May 1895 before the first L&SWR train arrived in Wadebridge. At around the same time the L&SWR was busy buying shares in the Exeter & Crediton and Taw Vale schemes. By using nominees, in both cases, the shareholders meetings were persuaded to reject terms offered by the Bristol & Exeter for working their lines and accept better terms offered by the L&SWR. The Bristol &Exeter and the Exeter & Crediton complained to the Railway Commissioners about the circumstances surrounding the rejection of the lease and, after some wrangling, the L&SWR were found guilty of malpractice but no sanctions were imposed, both lines subsequently opening as broad gauge.

Given the events outlined above, the broad gauge camp should have had a clear understanding of the South Western's intention to eventually build a line into North Devon and Cornwall, by using their recent converts to the "narrow gauge" cause as a spring board. The South Western also clearly stated in their evidence to the railway commissioners that it was their intention to do so. For the record it was to be July 1860 before the L&SWR arrived at Exeter Queen Street and February 1862 before the line down the hill to St. Davids and the mixed gauge on to Crediton via Cowley Bridge Junction were ready for use. Relations with the Great Western and the Bristol and Exeter had improved by 1875, when what was described by the historian of the Great Western Railway 'MacDermot' as the 'unpleasant incident of the take over of the Somerset & Dorset' occurred. The part played by the Somerset & Dorset in the Southern story is dealt with separately, but it is easy to see why so many of the L&SWR directors and management team went on to similar roles with the new Southern Railway.

By comparison with the L&SWR the London Brighton and South Coast Railway would appear as a timid little concern but this was far from the case. Stories of the Brighton holding off South Western at Havant are the stuff of legend but it was not quite what it seams. The Portsmouth direct line (as it is known today) was built as a speculative venture, by the contractor Thomas Brassey, with the intention of persuading the L&SWR to take it over. Initially the L&SWR showed little interest and the SE&CR were approached, they refused on the basis that it would be in breach of their agreement with the LB&SCR. The L&SWR then decided to take it on and ran a train down the line on 28 December 1858 only to find that a gang of LB&SCR men had removed the rails at Havant Junction and chained an engine to the track, after a brief struggle the obstructions were removed but progress was thwarted, when a little further on more rails had been removed and further fighting broke out. The matter was then referred to the courts and the first train finally ran on 24 January 1859. Eventually it was agreed that the section of line between Havant and Portcreek Junction should become jointly owned together with the section from Portcreek to Portsmouth, which had been already for the previous ten years.

As can be seen from the above account, the LB&SCR had a different philosophy to the Southern Railway's other constituent companies, in that it preferred to maintain reasonable relations with its neighbours but was not prepared to be walked on. From the earliest days LB&SCR's prosperity was built on the London area suburban traffic and not on the main line services to Brighton and along the coast to Eastbourne and Worthing as many people believe. It was to be well in to the Southern era before the coastal traffic outstripped the suburban as the main money spinner. Like most railways it also had its financial problems. By 1867, however, the Brighton's finances were in such a state that, following the departure of three chairmen in quick succession, the board appointed Samuel Laing to the post for a second time. He had been chairman from 1848 – 1855 resigning to take up a post in India. On his return he was again appointed to the post, serving for a further 19 years until 1896. He quickly got expenditure under control and sorted out the problems. Thereafter the LB&SCR was always careful with money and it was the prudent Brighton that provided the chief accountant and commercial manager to the newly formed Southern Railway.

Following a number of accidents in the early years, the Brighton pioneered the introduction of safety measures, including the provision of signals at junctions, Bricklayers' Arms Junction being the first in 1843. The signals provided were of a very rudimentary nature with hand signals by day and lamps by night and, of course, not interlocked. But an interlocking frame by John Saxby was brought into use during 1856 (almost certainly the first). The company stated in 1877 that it intended to adopt the Westinghouse air brake, and again, it was probably the first line of any size to have all its passenger trains equipped with continuous brakes.

Turning now to the SE&CR, or to give it its full title, the "South Eastern and Chatham Railway joint managing committee", the arrangements put in place were somewhat similar to those for the operation of a joint line. The SE&CR took over the day to day operations of the South Eastern Railway and the London Chatham & Dover Railway with effect from 1 January 1899, in advance of the approval of parliament, which was obtained on 5 August 1899. Each company nominated four directors to the new board, the net receipts being divided 59% to the SER and 41% to LC&DR. There had been a number of attempts in the early years to effect working union of the two companies. One was even approved by the directors of both companies, only to miss the parliamentary deadline, the following year it was thrown out by the LC&DR board. Nothing more was done, after the appointment of James Staats Forbes in 1861 as general manager and later, in 1873, as chairman of LC&DR. From 1861, for almost 40 years until the retirement of Sir Edward Watkin chairman of the SER, both companies maintained a sparring relationship, each somewhat distrusting of the other and there were a fair few skirmishes along the way.

Both the LC&DR and the SER built most of their lines as double track from the outset, rather than the more usual practice of acquiring enough land for double track and then building the line as single, often with the bridges and other structures built to take a second line. It was mostly the speculative lines that were originally single line only, that from Sevenoaks (later Bat & Ball) to Maidstone being an example. It was opened from Sevenoaks via Vestry South and East Junctions, to Maidstone as a single track in June 1874, the double tracking to Maidstone being completed by July 1883. The major problem with the railways in Kent and parts of East Sussex is that they were built on the cheap and to the minimum tolerances that could be got away with, generating much upgrading work in later years. All the railways of the Southern group suffered from this in one way or another. The effects of corner cutting were most commonly seen in speed and weight restrictions. In the case of the SER, this extended to the length and width of the vehicles permitted to use certain sections of the network. In later years this resulted in the provision of special rolling stock for use on these sections.

Much of the point scoring between the LC&DR and the SER concerned the carriage of mails between Dover and Calais. Prior to 1864 neither the SER nor LC&DR were empowered to operate steamships. The contract for the mails was let to Messrs Jenkins and Churchwood in 1854 who owned a small fleet of steamships. The rail portion of the journey was provided by the SER. In 1862 the LC&DR obtained the mail contract, subsequently subletting the sea crossing to Mr Churchward, who by now appeared to be on his own. This put the SER's nose out of joint, as they regarded the carriage of mails as their preserve. A deal was eventually done and the mails were carried jointly after June 1863. The steamships were purchased from Mr Churchward by the LC&DR after the necessary powers were obtained in 1864 and a pooling arrangement for the traffic was put in place in 1866. This was really the beginnings of the railways serious involvement in cross channel shipping activities and the development of Dover and Folkestone as ports. Following on from this spat both companies kept their distance, with the LC&DR entrenched at Dover and the service to Calais, the SER concentrating efforts at Folkestone and the route to Boulogne. After the formation of the SE&CR in 1899 there was some rationalisation of cross channel services, with many of the older ships being sold on or scrapped. Even the retained boats did not last that long, as the SE&CR was amongst the first to invest in the new generation of fast modern turbine driven ships, the first, "Queen", was ordered in 1902. The LB&SCR was not that far behind, with their first turbine driven ship the "Brighton" being launched the day after the "Queen's" sea trials. Both the LB&SCR and the L&SWR operated cross channel ferry services from various ports but as the sea crossings were much further, these routes were less popular. By the time the Southern railway was formed in 1923 most of the old ships had gone, thus endowing the new concern with a fleet of fast modern passenger ships.

Apart from companies mentioned in the original amalgamation act, there was one other railway that played an important role in the fledging Southern Railway and a very important role in the L&SWR's affairs before that. It was the Somerset and Dorset Joint Railway (S&DJR) in which the L&SWR had a half share, the other partner being firstly the Midland Railway (MR) and, after the grouping, the London Midland & Scottish Railway (LMS). You would think that with an eventual total of just 102 miles it wouldn't be that significant but it was, of course, of great strategic value to both its owners because it joined the standard gauge networks of the industrial Midlands, to those in the south and west, in the process gaining access to the ports and industry there, without having to tranship goods into broad gauge wagons, to get through the broad gauge area. As mentioned earlier it all came to a head in 1875. The Somerset & Dorset Railway was formed in 1862 by the amalgamation of the Dorset Central and the Somerset Central. At that time the Dorset Central was building its standard gauge line northwards from Wimborne towards Templecombe, not completed until 1863. The first section as far as Blandford was opened in 1860 and worked by the L&SWR. The Somerset Central on the other hand was busy building its initially broad gauge line (later mixed) from Burnham-on-Sea to Templecombe. It was mixed gauge as far as Bruton (actually Cole), where a connecting broad gauge spur was built to join the GWR line from Frome to Yeovil but apparently never used.

Following the amalgamation of the two companies as the Somerset and Dorset in 1862 all efforts were concentrated on building a line northwards over the Mendips to join the MR at Mangotsfield. Eventually in 1871 an act was obtained to build a line from Evercreech to Bath, to meet the MR branch from Mangotsfield to

*The modern LBSCR. A three-car South London line set at what may well be Battersea Park. The electric service on this route commenced on 1st December 1909.*

Bath, which had opened the previous year. The line to Bath opened in 1874 but the cost of building it brought the company to its knees, so that the obvious solution was to try to sell it. The S&D first approached the GWR, who for some reason, really only wanted the section north of Bruton. The GWR then made the mistake of offering the section south of Templecombe to the L&SWR. This must have set alarm bells ringing at Waterloo, as Archibald Scott the General Manager, was dispatched to see the MR people at Derby. Following a hastily arranged joint inspection of the line the L&SWR and the MR put forward an offer to lease the line. As the terms offered were somewhat better than those of the GWR, they were quickly accepted by the Somerset and Dorset board, the L&SWR and the MR taking over the line on a 999 year lease on 1 November 1875. After robust representations from the GWR as to a breach of faith on the part of the L&SWR, and the breach of an agreement with the MR not to extend beyond Bath, the lease was approved by parliament on 13 July 1876. Much to the relief of all concerned, the Joint Line was born and a standard gauge through route to the north was secured. Just how important this connection was can be gained from the fact that, in the first twelve months of operation of the new line to Bath, approximately 118,000 tons of goods passed over the line and onto MR metals at Bath Junction and that was just the beginning.

It remains to mention that in 1923 Parliamentary powers were obtained to transfer the Somerset and Dorset Joint Railway, which was still on lease, jointly to the London Midland & Scottish Railway and the Southern Railway. The act also allowed the Southern Railway to acquire the Lynton and Barnstaple line. Neither of these two lines was included in the 1921 act, as it did not cover joint or narrow gauge lines.

We must now look at another very important ingredient in the mix that became the Southern Railway. That is the subject of its connections and relations with other lines. Once again, history takes a hand as to the options available to the new organisation. The LB&SCR generally routed their traffic to and from the north of the country via London, Norwood Yard in the case goods and the West London Extension (WLE). It should be noted that the first 5 miles of the WLE were jointly owned by the L&NWR, GWR, LB&SCR and the L&SWR. The 2.½

*Ashley road Bridge - Walton-On-Thames looking west 7th August 1911. The train is on the Down Local line and headed by one of the small wheeled Drummond 4-4-0s. It is probably a stopping service. This section of the South western main line was widened to four tracks in 1903. The sidings opposite are perhaps better known as Oatlands carriage sidings.*

miles of the adjoining West London were owned jointly by the L&NWR and the GWR.

The SE&CR used the Metropolitan Widened Lines for much of the traffic travelling to the east coast, particularly that originating from the north Kent area, the WLE being favoured for traffic to the L&NWR at Willesden Junction and the west coast main line. Traffic to the West Country and Wales travelled west via Redhill and Guildford, to reach the Great Western at Reading, the SE&CR enjoying much better relations with the GWR than the L&SWR.

For the L&SWR the options were somewhat different. London area freights before the grouping originated from such diverse places as Nine Elms, Strawberry Hill and Wimbledon. After 1922, the new hump yard at Feltham came into use, with most of the north bound traffic then routed over the North London Line via Acton. Traffic from Southampton Docks and the Portsmouth area tended to be routed via Basingstoke and Reading or Salisbury for GWR destinations, the Midland and South West Junction (M&SWJR) line to Cheltenham being the preferred choice for destinations on the MR, rather than the Didcot Newbury and Southampton line which was owned by the GWR, probably to maximise the L&SWR's mileage. Direct traffic for the L&NW and East Coast travelled to London, before heading north over the WLE. Goods traffic originating in the West Country and heading for destinations in the north was routed through Templecombe and on to the S&D as a matter of policy. Most north bound traffic from the Bournemouth and Poole areas was also routed on to the S&D, via Wimborne or Broadstone. Prior to 1923 both the L&SWR and the MR went to great lengths to route as much traffic as possible via the S&D and the M&SWJR, to avoid having to pay the GWR a share of the revenue.

Having now looked at the diverse organisations that formed the new Southern Railway, together with some of the relevant history and the baggage that accompanied it, Part Two will take a look at "The Inheritance" and examine just what each of them brought to the party by way of assets, or in some cases otherwise.

*LBSCR turbine steamer 'Brighton' leaving Newhaven Harbour 3rd March 1904 on the Dieppe service. At about the same time telegraphic communication had been established between the two ports, following the erection of a mast and relay room at Newhaven Harbour. Photographs show a temporary rail line running alongside, which may well then have been used to assist in the construction.*

**Bibliography and Acknowledgements**

I would like to acknowledge the assistance and encouragement of the editor, in persuading me to produce this series of articles. Particular thanks are due to Martin Stone and my many other friends who have offered both assistance and guidance during the writing of this the first article in the series. The principle printed sources consulted are:

*The Somerset & Dorset Railway*
Robin Atthill. David & Charles 1967

*A History of the Southern Railway*
C F Dendy Marshall. Southern Railway 1936

*The Okehampton Line*
John Nicholas and George Reeve. Irwell Press 2001

*The Isle of Wight Railway*
R J Maycock & R Silbury. The Oakwood Press 1999

*The Isle of Wight Central Railway*
R J Maycock & R Silbury. The Oakwood Press 2001

*The Freshwater Yarmouth & Newport Railway*
J Maycock & R Silbury. The Oakwood Press 2003

*Isle of Wight Steam Passenger Rolling Stock*
R J Maycock & M J E Reed. The Oakwood Press 1997

*An Illustrated History of the North Cornwall Railway*
David Roe. Irwell Press 1995

*The North Devon Line*
John Nicolas. OPC 1992

*Britain's Joint Lines*
H C Casserley. Ian Allan 1968

# SMOKE GETS IN YOUR EYES

Victoria, 14th September 1908 — John Minnis

These three photographs are official LB&SCR views, taken to show how the newly-installed signals outside Victoria on Grosvenor bank were obscured by smoke. One of them, that of I1 class 4-4-2Ts Nos. 1 and 3, was used by the late R. C. Riley in Brighton Line Album (1967) but the other two are previously unpublished. Although taken to illustrate a particular operating problem, they reveal much that is interesting to us in the way of rolling stock and train workings.

**Above** - The two I1s are both immaculate with No. 3 waiting to back down on to an awaiting train and No. 1 at the head of a Hastings excursion. The train for the latter is formed of Stroudley 4 wheel coaches made up of two 7 coach sets and is one of the very few examples of these being recorded in the brown and cream Marsh livery. Only sets made up for excursion duties seem to have been so favoured. In the right background, a train of ex LC&DR stock can be seen on the Chatham side of the station.

**Opposite top -** On the left, Victoria Shunting box was built in 1906 and, although closed in 1939, survived as shunters' accommodation until the 1970s. An unidentified Billinton E5 0-6-2T on a rake of Stroudley 4 wheel coaches passes a Stroudley D1 0-4-2T. Through the arches of the bridge can just be glimpsed the engine sidings and turntable.

**Opposite bottom** - A Billinton radial tank draws its train, the first two vehicles of which are a covered carriage truck and a bogie third, in the Marsh livery. On the left is something that must have been frequently seen, yet was very rarely photographed. A D1 is shunting some through stock, that must have been worked round via the West London Extension Railway. The nearest two vehicles are from the Midland Railway, a 20ft milk van to D416, one of 120 built 1881-93, which were fitted with torpedo vents from around 1904 and a 31ft 6 wheel motor car van to D414, one of 25 built in 1906. These are the only two vehicles in the train that can be positively identified. The coach under the bridge is largely obscured but its profile suggests it might be GNR.

# SMOKE GETS IN YOUR EYES

***Above -** Uniquely amongst the four pre-nationalisation companies, the SR had the distinction of being the only concern not to have installed water troughs, as per the invention of John Ramsbottom in 1861. Certainly they had been discussed, by the LSWR at least, in the early of the present century, but it was not until the 1948 interchange trials that SR men were faced with the opportunity to try out what the others had been using for more than half a century. Seen above is 34006 'Bude', recorded at Brighton, complete with LMS tender (fitted with water pick-up gear), ready to take part in the interchange trials of that year.*

***Below -** An 'S15' leaving Basingstoke yard after what was perhaps the average 6 minute water stop for through goods workings. It was delays such as this, that the installation of troughs near Farnborough would hopefully avoid.*

# WATER TROUGHS ON THE SOUTHERN

## From notes provided by Tony Hillman

Unique amongst the 'Big Four' and indeed also amongst the regions of British Railways, the Southern never provided water troughs anywhere on its system. An amount of correspondence about the reasons for this and the options considered over the years has been published elsewhere, although, suffice to say that the situation had always been that the lengths of non-stop run involved were not considered as sufficient justification for such an installation. Indeed, the prime candidate for a non-stop run had always been the West of England services, the 'Devon Belle' being forced to make an un-timetabled stop at Wilton, west of Salisbury, in order to provide a fully watered engine. In this respect the SR Exeter services could never compete with those running from Paddington, whilst any suggestion an even longer non-stop workings, Waterloo to Plymouth or Ilfracombe, would have been even more restricted, not just by water supplies but also due to restrictions on the types of locomotive that might be used.

As mentioned at the start of this article, we know the subject of water troughs have been discussed in past years but we are not aware of copies of any of the actual correspondence having come to light previously. It was therefore a delight to be offered a copy of the 1948 'Report of Department set up to consider the provision of Water Troughs', kindly loaned to us by Tony Hillman and which is reproduced in full.

**" 1 - REMIT**

The Chief Regional Officer's letter of 6th January asked for a joint report to be prepared on the question of the provision of water troughs between London and Exeter by the Chief Civil Engineer, Chief Mechanical Engineer and Superintendent of Operation. Mr Smart to take the initiative.

The joint report to have regard to the particular circumstances in this region under which, at present, only one train 'The Devon Belle', could definitely require to use the water troughs. At the same time, the mechanical and operational advantages of using water troughs should be fully set out together with details of the amount of time, labour and materials etc. that the project would involve and the estimated initial and maintenance costs.

A further letter from the Chief Regional Officer dated 6th February advised that the committee should, '.......confine their enquiries to the Western Section, at any rate for the time being'.

Regard should also be paid to the possibility of the introduction of some other form of motive power, such as electric and / or diesel locomotives within a few years.

**"2 - REPORT**

Investigations have been completed and the following report is submitted.

**"3 - SELECTION OF ROUTES**

It is considered that in the Western Section the only routes appropriate to the provision of water troughs are as follows: Waterloo to Exeter, Waterloo to Weymouth, Portsmouth to Salisbury (via Redbridge).

**"4 SITES SELECTED**

The small number of sites where a sufficient length of track is level has been examined having regard to operating requirements, water supply, drainage facilities and obstructions such as level crossings.

The most suitable sites are as follows:

a - Between Farnborough and Fleet (33m. 51½ch. To 34m. 8ch.) Four running lines would be involved, i.e. Down Fast, Down Slow, Up Fast, and Up Slow. The site would enable all passenger and freight trains between the London area and Eastleigh, Southampton and Bournemouth and Weymouth on the one hand and West of England on the other to take water at an appropriate distance from London and before reaching Worting Junction, the point at which the West of England and Weymouth lines diverge.

b - Between Millborne Port and Sherbourne (114m. 68½ch. to 115m. 25ch.) There are two running lines at this spot. This would serve as a second picking up point on the London / West of England and Portsmouth / West of England routes.

c - Between Millbrook and Redbridge (80m. 69ch. to 81m. 25½ch.) There are four running lines at this spot but two of these are lines from the Docks and are excluded. The site would serve as a second picking up point for the London - Weymouth route and also serve the Portsmouth - Salisbury route. This is the only possible site between Worting Junction and Bournemouth.

**"5. SPEED OF TRAINS**

It has been ascertained from the other Regions that water can be picked up at all speeds from about 20 mph upwards. The most satisfactory range is from 45 to 50 mph. Actual speeds of representative trains over the suggested sites have been recorded and normally fulfil these conditions.

**"6. DENSITY OF TRAFFIC**

Based on the 1948 train service and Saturday 24th July 1948 in particular, the following details are given of the traffic passing the three suggested sites:-

| | Farnborough (4 lines) | Milborne Port (2 lines) | Millbrook (2 lines) |
|---|---|---|---|
| **Total number of trains per annum** | 50,205 | 23,898 | 40,968 |
| **Average number of trains per weekday (Summer)** | 143 | 71 | 123 |
| **Actual number of trains on Saturday, 24th July 1948 (peak day)** | 209 | 92 | 178 |

| | Farnborough | Milborne Port | Millbrook |
|---|---|---|---|
| **Assumed Average Number of Trains per hour** | 18 | 5 | 9 |
| **Average Hourly rate of supply from Troughs to Engines, allowing for spillage** | 25,000 gls./hr. | 12,500 gls./hr. | 22,500 gls./hr. |
| **Total requirement in 24 hours (Saturday peak)** | 600,000 galls. | 500,00 galls. | 540,000 galls. |
| **Assumed daily delivery of water from mains** | 200,000 galls. | 150,000 galls. | 240,000 galls. |
| **Storage required to cope with Saturday Summer peak** | 400,000 galls. | 150,000 galls. | 300,000 galls. |

**"7. CONSUMPTION OF WATER**

Details of the required flow of water and of the storage required have been estimated from the details of the train service on a peak Saturday and on the assumption that each train picks up 2,000 gallons and that 500 gallons are lost by spillage.

Note - Tentative enquiries from the local Water Authorities indicate that there will at times be severe restrictions on their rate of supply and this will have to be taken care of by the provision of adequate storage to cope with peak demands. The Maximum hourly rate of demand may easily exceed the supply by a considerable amount, but the storage has been estimated on the assumption that deficiencies in supply will be made up at times convenient to the Water Authority. It is anticipated that in the event of firm proposals being put forward the Water Authorities will make every endeavour to meet the requirement.

**"8. CONSTRUCTION OF STORAGE TANKS AND TROUGHS**

A storage tank would be provided at each site, from which each trough would be separately supplied through a pipe-line, and the filling up of the troughs would be controlled by float valves situated in a valve house adjacent to the storage tank.

Owing to the restricted site conditions and the heavy peak demand in relation to the rate of supply available at each site, the storage tank would have to be very long and narrow, probably of reinforced concrete, supported on the side of the slope of the embankment (at Farnborough) or the cutting (at Milbourne Port and Millbrook) by reinforced concrete piles or piers.

The troughs would probably consist of 10 ft. rolled steel sections welded into 60 ft. lengths and bolted together with rubber packings. The troughs would be supported on the sleepers on wrought iron brackets. They would be supplied from the storage tanks by 8" diameter cast iron pipes. The length would be 800 yards including a 60 yard ramp at either end.

**"9. SPILLAGE AND RECOVERY OF WATER**

Enquiries from other regions indicate that allowance must be made for the spillage of 40% of the water supplied to the troughs. Special provision would be made to recover as much spilled water as possible by providing a drainage system of concrete slabs (which would also serve to prevent stone ballast from being thrown up), channels, catch pits on drain tanks, from which it would be pumped back to the storage tank.

*Urie rebuild, No 336 at an unreported location but likely to be approaching Basingstoke from the south. Tantalisingly save for the suggestion that new build steam locomotives should be automatically fitted with water pick-up gear, as indeed the standard classes were, there is no definite detail as to which of the existing SR types would be retro-fitted. 'Pacifics' working on the Western Section would certainly be included, but so then might members of the 'Lord Nelson', 'N15', 'S15', 'H15', 'Schools' and even some of the 2-6-0 types. It would not have mattered whether the SR tenders to be converted were of the six or eight wheel type as both had been successfully fitted with water pick-up on other regions.*

**"10. WATER TREATMENT**

In all three cases it will be necessary to purchase water from the local Water Authority, as none of the sites permits the introduction of a boring or other means of pumping water privately.

Allowance has been made for treatment of the water in all three cases so as to reduce the hardness to the requisite figure and the softening plants will be provided adjacent to the storage tanks.

**"11. ADAPTION OF LOCOMOTIVE TENDERS**

Assuming that it is decided to proceed with the installation of water troughs, then so far as locomotives are concerned it is recommended that the following two conditions should be fulfilled.

a - All new building, i.e. both tender and tank locomotives (except for a small variety of the latter) should be fitted with water pick up gear and tenders of appropriate coal and water capacity.

b - In addition, as a provisional estimate, some 250 existing passenger and freight locomotives now operating on the Western Section should be provided with water pick up apparatus. In this instance and in order to keep conversion costs to a minimum it is recommended that a substantial variation in tender coal and water capacity is not desirable.

**"12. FINANCIAL**

Capital Account, cost of construction

| | |
|---|---|
| Farnborough | £ 89,000 |
| Milborne Port | £ 47,000 |
| Millbrook | £ 52,000 |
| Adoption of 250 locomotive tenders @ £275 each | £ 68,750 |
| | £256,750 |

Revenue Account

| | |
|---|---|
| Maintenance of plant | £1,700 |
| Additional Track maintenance | £3,100 |

Annual cost of Water Supply including pumping and treatment:

| | |
|---|---|
| Farnborough | £14,075 |
| Milborne Port | £ 6,095 |
| Millbrook | £ 9,190 |
| Net cost of water supply by trough per annum: | £29,360 |
| | |
| Estimated cost of water, if supplied as now at Nine Elms, Waterloo, Salisbury and Exeter (per annum): | £11,500 |
| Increased cost due to troughs: | £17,060 |
| Interest on capital at 4%: | £10,270 |
| Total | £32,930 |

**"13. COMPLETION TIME**

It is estimated that provided materials are available the work of constructing the water troughs and storage tanks and of adapting the locomotive tenders could be completed within two years from the date of authorisation.

**"14. ADVANTAGES**

a - The installation of Water Troughs at the sites mentioned will enable non stop runs between such points as London and Exeter (including of course the 'Devon Belle) to be introduced as may be found desirable. This could be applicable to both Passenger and Freight Trains.

*In accordance with the timetable in existence at the time the report was compiled, the only obvious non-stop service was the 'Devon Belle', whether it was indeed operational difficulties that precluded the introduction of other similar workings, or a throw back to the Salisbury disaster of 1906, that made the SR wary of non-stop workings through Salisbury, we shall never know. With hindsight the comments made relative to difficulties with the rostering of men and machines may appear strange to understand, but it must be recalled that in 1948 the flexibility and utilisation that diesel traction would offer had yet to be realised, this would become only too apparent with 10201-3 within a very short timescale. Unfortunately full utilisation of these modern machines was never gained, due to the failure to slot them into working schedules still restricted by steam. The newly created Southern Region were also in 1948 still unsure as to which direction modernisation would take, would it still be the implementation of the Southern Railway modernisation plan of 1946, in which steam would have had life of little more than 10 years? As it was troughs were never provided and steam lasted almost a further 20 years from 1948. An opportunity was thus lost to afford a more efficient service to rival that from Paddington, certainly in so far as trains serving the West Country. Passengers might also have benefited in other ways, services being able to start to the west not just from Waterloo and then running non-stop through Salisbury, but perhaps also from Salisbury, this way overcrowding might have been avoided and who knows - the railway remained more attractive for longer. Seen here is a busy time at Seaton Junction with the passenger service identified as the 9.35 am to Exeter Central behind 34081 '92 Squadron'.*

*J H Aston*

b - The elimination of the present practice of changing engines at such points as Salisbury and Bournemouth could provide a more flexible basis on which engine diagrams could be compiled. The exact effect of this in terms of economy in engine workings and man power - it is unlikely to be very much - cannot be determined at this stage. It is possible to say, however, that the elimination of the bulk of engine changing at Salisbury on such occasions as Summer Saturdays could be of considerable local benefit to traffic operation.

c - The existence of water troughs on this Region could enable other Regions' locomotives to work our main line traffic. Conversely if our locomotives were fitted with water pick-up apparatus they could work long distance non-stop traffic on other Regions. Furthermore, standardisation of locomotive design on an inter-regional basis would be facilitated.

d - Occasional delays at such stations as Southampton Central by engines taking water should be eliminated.

e - Eleven booked freight trains and special freight trains from Southampton Docks to Nine Elms now scheduled to call at Basingstoke for about 6 minutes each would not now need to do so.

f - A slight saving in coal consumption would eventually be achieved in the case of new tenders designed expressly to pick up water from troughs (Because of the small reduction in overall weight of the tender) but not in the case of the existing tenders which would have to be adapted.

**15. DISADVANTAGES**

a - Engine Working. The through running of engines between London and Exeter would counteract the efforts constantly made to keep specific pairs of men to their own engines, unless 'lodging away' were re-introduced. This step might be strongly resisted by the Trade Unions although it may be noted that the Railway Executive are known to be anxious to increase the present scale of 'lodging turns' on Regions other than our own. Incidentally, the train service would not permit of a locomotive making a round trip London - Exeter - London, except in a few cases and less miles per engine per day might be difficult to avoid.

b - Track Maintenance. The constant spilling of water on the track is very detrimental to maintenance; although as mentioned earlier in this report about 60% of the spilled water might be recovered by an efficient drainage system, the remainder soaks through the ballast into the formation, which in time may become waterlogged. This condition encourages weed growth and may make the maintenance of an accurate top (such as is required to avoid wastage of water over the edge of the trough at a low place) an unduly labourous task.

The difficulty is enhanced by the fact that the ballast chippings become scoured out from under the sleepers.

Packing is, therefore, more frequently required, but is impeded by the presence of slabs which have to be provided in order to prevent stones from being thrown up. These slabs have to be drawn out under the rail and replaced every time a sleeper has to be packed.

The life of the track may be reduced to about one half of its normal life owing to the wastage of rails by corrosion and by abrasion and excessive chair cutting of the sleepers.

Thus, relaying become necessary at more frequent intervals with the added inconvenience of removing the

*For some strange reason, views of the up 'ACE' appear rare, although here the engine of the London service, 35004 'Cunard White Star', is recorded leaving Waterloo - light, and making its way back to Nine Elms. Alongside is 34108 'Wincanton'. The 'ACE' would certainly have been another service to benefit from water-troughs.*

*Mick Uden collection*

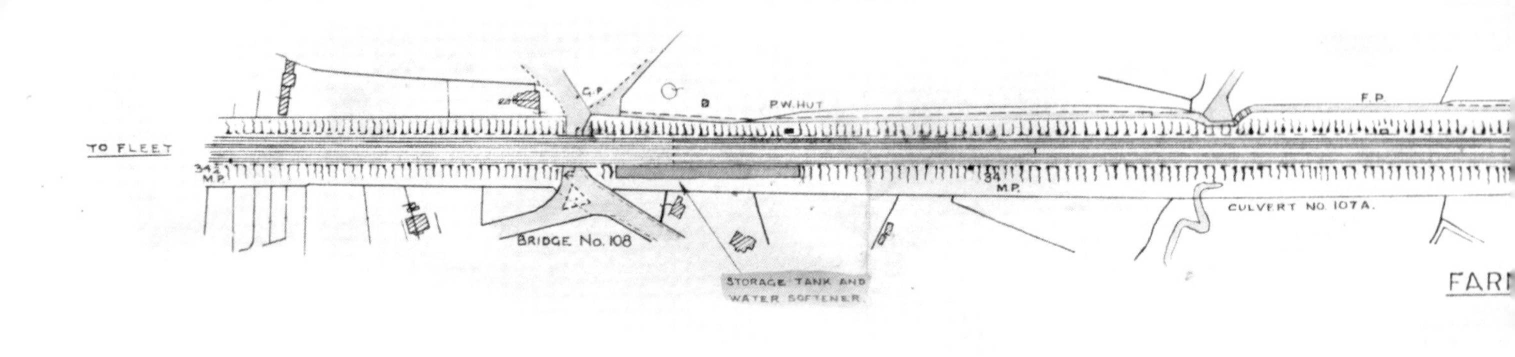


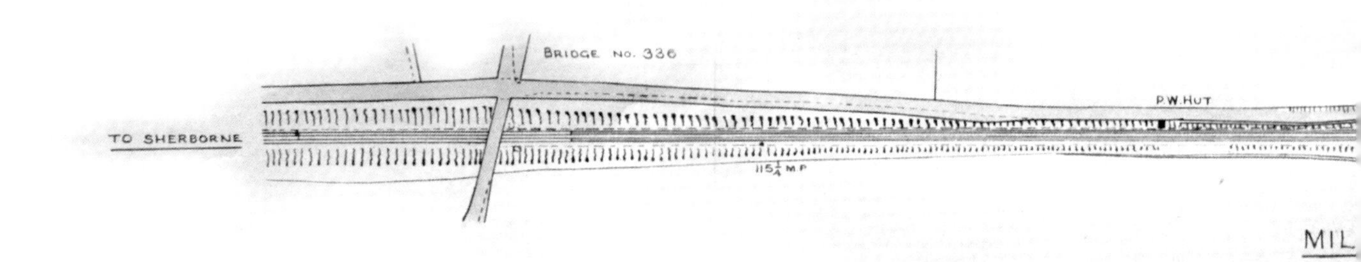


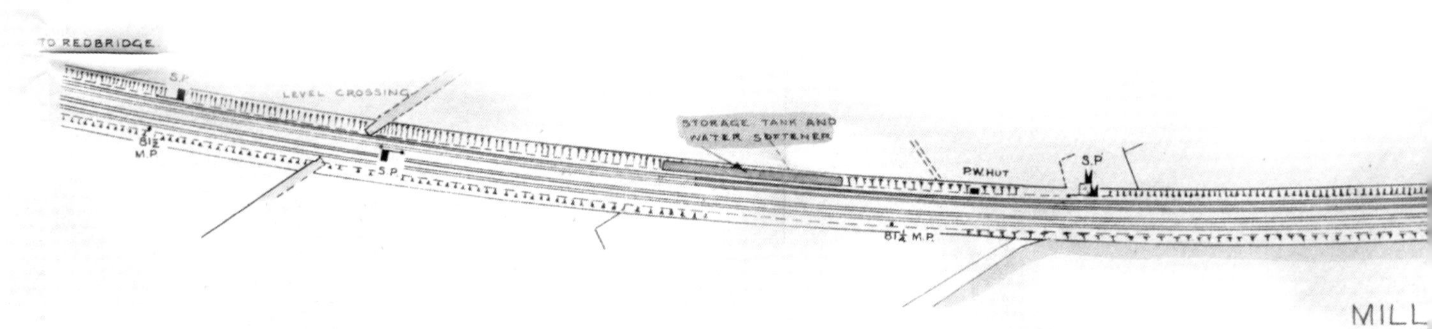

*Water storage of a smaller type. The storage facility at Colyton on the Seaton Branch, recorded on 4th May 1959.*

*A E West.*

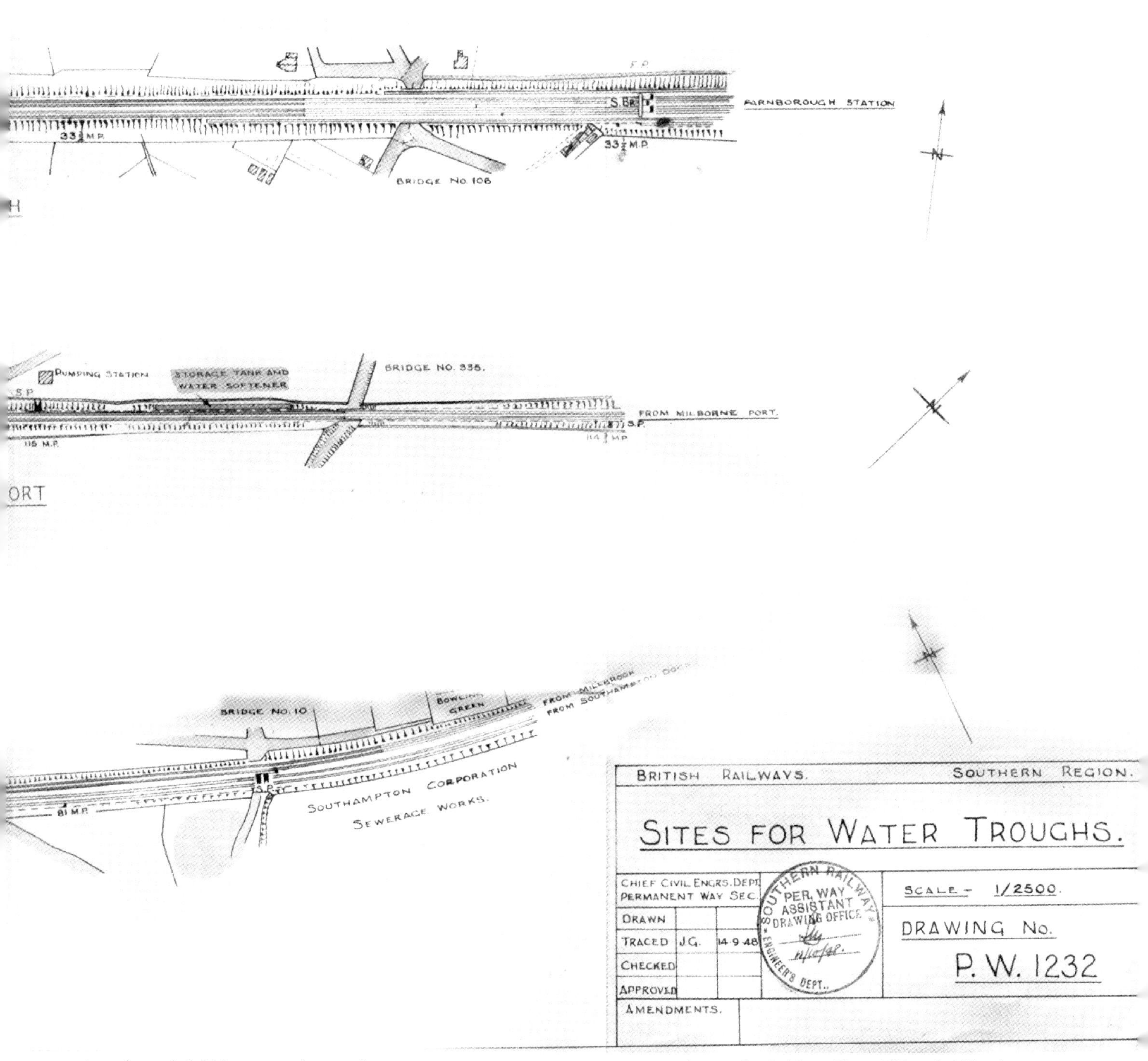


troughs and slabbing on each occasion.

The tracks become ice-bound and very slippery in the winter and the work of inspecting and keeping the troughs clear of ice is distinctly dangerous under such conditions.

c - Other Considerations. The wet condition of the track is unfavourable to the maintenance of track circuits.

Whilst the sites selected for the troughs fulfil the essential requirements, it has not been possible to locate them away from public roads and footpaths.

The installation of troughs might result in complaints from the users of these roads and footpaths, of inconvenience due to the excessive splashing (such as may occur when a tender is overfilled), particularly from any persons passing under bridges Nos. 107 and 108 when a down train is taking water or passing under bridges Nos. 106 , 107 and 355 when an up train is taking water.

**"16. CONCLUSION**

In our opinion the problem may be summed up in the following terms:

a - There are no technical or physical considerations that would prevent the installation of Water Troughs on the principal Western Section routes of this Region. Certain disadvantages, mainly in regard to maintenance, would attend such a step, but none of these are prohibitive.

b - From the operating point of view the main advantage

would be to work non-stop such trains as the 'Devon Belle'. Apart from this aspect while there are, it is true, certain other operating advantages, none of these appear to be of decisive importance.

c - It must be borne in mind that if the introduction of Main line Electrification or Diesel locomotives (or other prime movers such as Gas Turbine locomotives) is regarded as a possibility on the Western Section in the not too distant future, then all the operating advantages already mentioned could be accomplished without the attendent disadvantages.

If in the meantime, Water Troughs have been installed they would then become a liability rather than an asset during the period that steam locomotives remain in limited use and ultimately they would be of no further use whatsoever.

d - Our conclusion is, therefore, that there can be no justification for the provision of Water Troughs unless both the following questions can be answered in the affirmative:

i - Will the steam locomotive remain the principal form of motive power on the Western Section for, say, at least ten years after Water Troughs have been brought into use?

ii - Is the importance attached to such trains as the 'Devon Belle' and to the other advantages already recited sufficient to justify the expenditure that has been indicated?"

This committee had not in its possession information which would enable it to answer these two questions satisfactorily. It therefore feels that it can best discharge its function by setting out the facts and then submitting these problems of policy for decision.

(Although the names of the committee members were not reported, it is known that they represented four departments, The Superintendent of Operation, Superintendent of Motive Power, two from the Chief Civil Engineer and the Chief Mechanical Engineer.)

*It is doubtful if the Southern Region would have retro-fitted any of its tank engines, indeed in 1948 they had none that were being used for main line services - a definite throwback to Sevonoaks and 1927. Seem here is a potential candidate for taking advantage of water-troughs, the Portsmouth - Cardiff service, which, on 18th August 1953, was in charge of 'U' 31796, leaving Southampton Central with a formation that included both LMR and WR stock. To be fair, most of these services at the time called at Southampton Central anyway, so the benefit of troughs at Redbridge for these workings was limited. The same would have applied to the Brighton - Bournemouth and Brighton - Plymouth workings. Redbridge troughs would have come into their own if a non-stop Bournemouth working had been introduced. (No 31796 had originally been built as a 2-6-4T and carried the name 'River Stour'.)*

*Les Elsey*

***Above*** *- From the vantage point of the coaling plant at Exmouth Junction, a birds-eye view of the shed is obtained. At least nine locomotives of various types are visible, although who knows what others were lurking both within and thereabouts? Three can be identified by number, 1795, 21C25 'Whimple' and 1407. The importance of Exmouth Junction as a main depot may well have increased with troughs installed, as locomotives from Nine Elms would have become regular visitors, the 'Merchant Navy' type not being permitted to venture further west onto the former LSWR lines to Ilfracombe or Plymouth. 29th June 1948.* *J H Aston*

***Right*** *- 'H2' 32422 'North Foreland' at Southampton Central on a Bournemouth - Brighton, working probably 1951. The fireman is filling the tank. It is doubtful whether any specific improvement in speed would have been achieved with this service by the installation of troughs at Redbridge and the conclusion is therefore reached that the report's comments over the potential benefit to these type of cross-country workings was negligible.*

# Terry Cole's Rolling Stock File No. 6

## Three Push-Pull Trains

Ex LBSCR stock has so far been conspicuous by its absence from these 'Files'. There is good reason for that. The LBSCR, although having superior systems such as overhead electrification and air braking, was the smallest company and most of its senior officers had taken retirement at the Grouping. Its coaching stock was also predominately of antiquated design and consequently was soon swept away under the Southern regime. The better stock was converted to suburban electric stock or sent to the Isle of Wight, where the air braking system remained in use. Electrification to the south coast and the arrival of new Maunsell stock cleared away any 'Balloon' mainline stock which remained. One of the LBSCR's 'innovations' did, however, survive and prosper. By 1910 they had realised that the economic operation of many secondary routes and local services lay with the locomotive hauled 'Motor trains'. As a consequence they started building and converting coaches specifically for these services. These were the LBSCR vehicles which were to survive in use on the mainland up till 1960. The Southern developed this idea converting many otherwise redundant coaches into 'push-pull' sets, these conversions continuing right up to 1960, with the production of 20 Maunsell push-pull sets to replace the pre-grouping survivors.

*Photo. 1 - above.* Here LBSCR set 724 (originally 991) is entering Brighton on $26^{th}$ September 1951 with a train from Steyning and Horsham. The nearest vehicle is S 3823 S an eight compartment Driving Brake $3^{rd}$ to diagram 188, one of four built in 1912 for the Eastbourne – St Leonard's services. Behind is S 6247 S, one of four composites built in 1922 to strengthen these sets. Set 724 was disbanded in 1953, with 3823 going on to see service on the Midhurst branch as a single coach, before being used on the restored services on the Bluebell line prior to final closure. It was finally condemned in 1960.

*Photo. 2 - opposite top.* The Southern soon found some redundant coaches in the shape of the eight ex SECR steam rail motors to convert into more push pull sets. These were rebuilt in 1924 into four 2-car sets: two articulated sets (one of which we saw in Rolling Stock File No 2) and two conventional push pull sets, originally destined for the Isle of Wight. Here is one of these two latter conversions, set 482 pictured at Westerham on $24^{th}$ September 1953 in BR red livery. They were not successful on the IOW and returned to the mainland in 1927. The set comprises saloon trailer third S 915 S, originally a composite to diagram 364 and saloon driving brake third S 3583 S to diagram 223. The set was withdrawn in 1960.

*Photo. 3 - below.* Amongst the many vehicles the Southern converted to push pull sets were 18 ex LSWR 'Emigrant' coaches. These interesting vehicles had originally been built from 1905, for the then lucrative traffic in emigrants entering this country from mainland Europe by the east coast ports and leaving for America from Southampton. In order to be able to travel over any company's routes they were built to a very restricted loading gauge and were only 46 ft 6 in long. The surviving 18 vehicles were converted in 1942/3 to form nine push pull sets, the resulting coaches being to four different diagrams. This photograph, taken at Paddock Wood on 18th August 1951 shows the Hawkhurst branch train. The leading vehicle has three doors on the corridor side, making it one of the two diagram 289 composites 4763-4 so this is either set 738 or 739. The rear driving third is either 2648 or 2649 to diagram 100. There will be more on these coaches in a future 'File'.

# WHITSTABLE HARBOUR

*For 120 years, until closure at the end of 1952, Whitstable Harbour was served by rail and shunted by railway horse. The line was, of course, part of the famous Canterbury & Whitstable railway, itself one of the earliest of the standard gauge lines. We present here two recently acquired views, that above from Roger Carpenter (the J W Sparrowe collection) shows part of the facilities at Easter 1939, whilst that below is a view from the collection of Irvine Cresswell.*

# BIRDS EYE VIEW

*The unseen Waterloo, prior to expansion for the now defunct Eurostar services. At first glance, the whole area appears to be little more than a dumping ground for various railway related stores. No doubt it would have yielded any number of fascinating older items, had the opportunity presented itself, or indeed we had been aware of the change that would overtake the railway system in the following few years. The lift to the 'Drain' is also apparent, the one where 'M7' No 672 came to grief in May 1948 and was promptly condemned and cut up. It cannot be denied the location was dingy. Dirt from decades of coal smoke, not just railway of course, had blackened the area to lie like a sticky mass over much of the infrastructure. The exception of course is the Exmouth Junction prefabricated hut, seemingly recently placed although its specific function is uncertain. Evidently taken outside of rush-hour, as the various 'SUB' and 'EPB' sets await the returning commuters.*

## 'TRAIN OF EVENTS'

*Another fascinating view that arrived with us, nothing written on the reverse as to a date and to be fair perhaps not of the best quality. We know it is Southampton Central and obviously the 'Merchant Navy', No 35021, has failed whilst at the head of the down ' Belle'. It is seen here waiting to be towed away, no doubt to Eastleigh. Shortage of steam would appear not to have been the problem, so what was it, injectors, a hot box, or the Bulleid valve gear / steam reverser.......?*

*Read on over the page......*

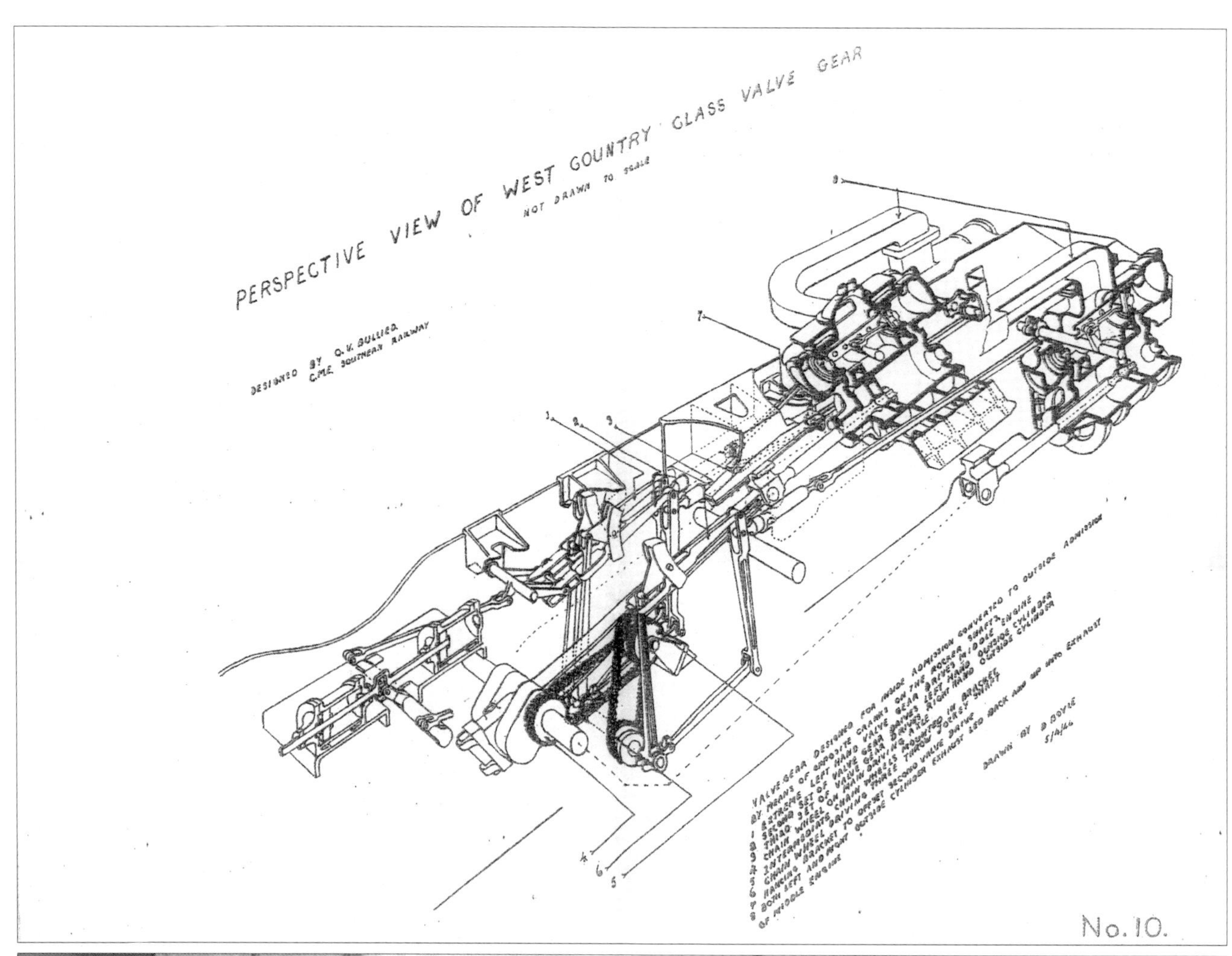
PERSPECTIVE VIEW OF WEST COUNTRY CLASS VALVE GEAR
NOT DRAWN TO SCALE
DESIGNED BY O.V. BULLIED.
C.M.E. SOUTHERN RAILWAY
VALVE GEAR DESIGNED FOR INSIDE ADMISSION CONVERTED TO OUTSIDE ADMISSION
BY MEANS OF OPPOSITE CRANKS ON THE ROCKER SHAFTS.
1 EXTREME LEFT HAND VALVE GEAR DRIVES MIDDLE ENGINE
2 SECOND SET OF VALVE GEAR DRIVES LEFT HAND OUTSIDE CYLINDER
3 THIRD SET OF VALVE GEAR DRIVES RIGHT HAND OUTSIDE CYLINDER
4 CHAIN WHEEL ON MAIN DRIVING AXLE
5 INTERMEDIATE CHAIN WHEELS MOUNTED IN BRACKET
6 CHAIN WHEEL DRIVING THREE THROW JOCKEY SHAFT
7 HANGING BRACKET TO OFFSET SECOND VALVE DRIVE
8 BOTH LEFT AND RIGHT OUTSIDE CYLINDER EXHAUST LED BACK AND UP INTO EXHAUST
OF MIDDLE ENGINE
DRAWN BY D BOYLE
5/4/46
No. 10.

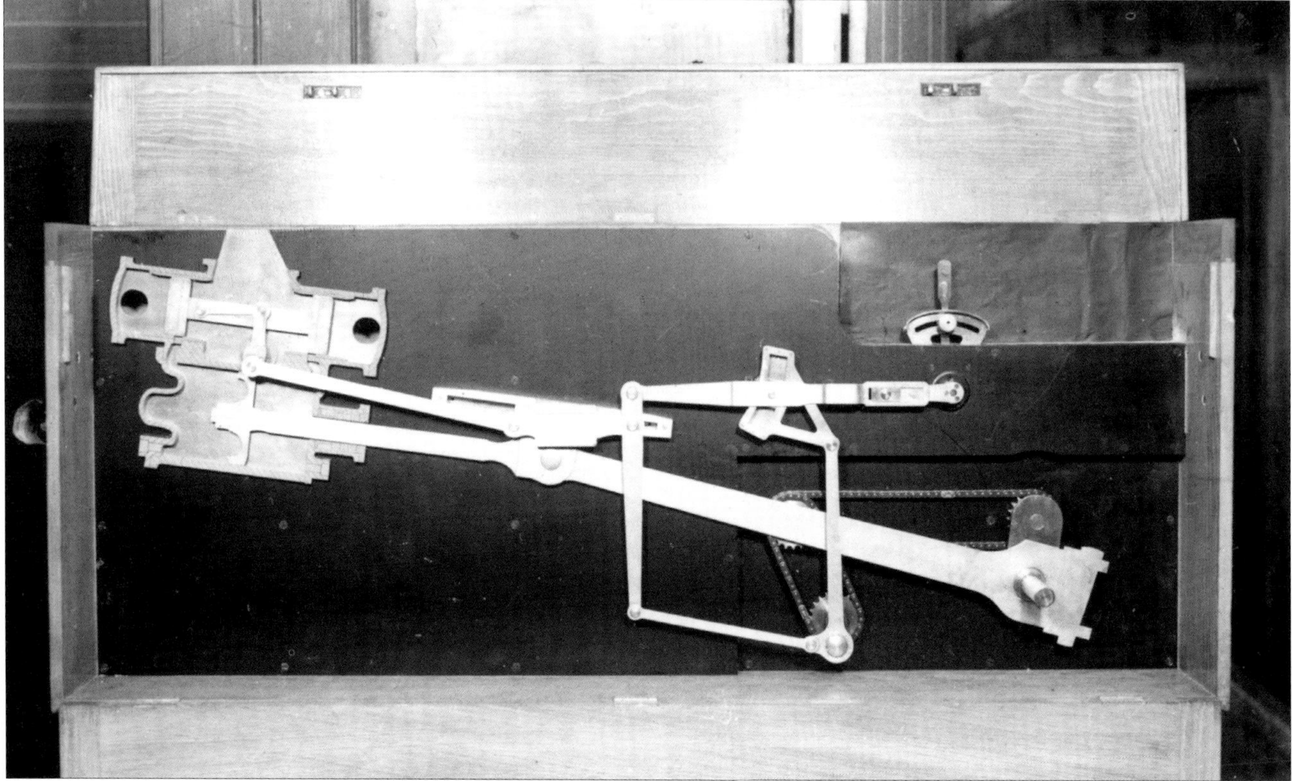

# The BULLEID STEAM REVERSER GEAR

## Martin Breakspear

Anybody who has had to operate a manual valve gear on a steam locomotive will know that, even with a screw reverser, a lot of effort is needed to continually link up or down, especially when shunting with constant reversals of direction. A pole reverser demands even more effort and is sometimes impossible to operate with full boiler pressure at the cylinders, even under normal operating conditions.

The Southern Railway Pacifics originally had boilers pressed to 280lbs per sq inch. Although this pressure can rarely have been seen at the cylinders especially with the engines' propensity to slip, the potential was there and even a screw reverser would have needed a lot of effort to move valves under that pressure. Under slip conditions it would have been almost impossible. The unfortunate experience with 'Blue Peter' demonstrates how things could get seriously out of control. Power operated valve control might have helped get things under control before much damage was done. A power operated system offers the advantage that direct linkage between the control levers and the valve gear could be unnecessary, giving flexibility in the design for the relative positions of the control and the gear.

The obvious source of power on a steam engine is clearly the steam itself. Various attempts to design power operated system were made, and the Southern had three; the LBSC design, the Eastleigh design, and finally the Bulleid design. No doubt Bulleid's vision of future steam locomotive design took account of the advantages of power operated valve gear and his openness to novelty in design must also have contributed to his decision to fit his design of gear to the Pacifies.

The three Southern designs shared common principles, and the variations came in the layout and controls.

The common principles were:

- The use of steam as the power source
- Use of hydraulic locking
- Remote and indirect control from the cab of the gear
- Remote and indirect indication in the cab of the gear's position

At first sight, the complete diagram of the system may look complicated to understand. Breaking it down into the four functions outlined above will simplify explanation.

**The Steam Cylinder,**

The power cylinder is a simple double acting cylinder. This means that steam pressure can be applied at either end of the cylinder to move the piston forwards and backwards over its entire stroke.

One end of the cylinder rod is connected to the weighshaft, or reverser shaft in Southern parlance. (See the diagram of the valve gear). This is the shaft that directly operates the valve gear on the engine. The type of valve gear used, (Walschaerts on the Pacifies) is irrelevant to the principle of operation of the power system. If steam is applied to one end of the cylinder, the piston moves to the other end and the engine is reversed. Applying steam to the other end moves the gear back into its original position. The non-powered end of the cylinder either exhausts the waste steam to atmosphere, or more likely, the steam condenses into water if infrequent changes in valve setting are made and is escapes by automatic cylinder drains underneath the engine.

The amount of power generated depends entirely upon the boiler pressure and the size of the cylinder, more pressure and bigger cylinders giving more power. There are therefore design compromises to be made as boiler pressure will vary during lighting up and during running, and the valve gear must be operable under all operational conditions from light steam shed movements to full load out on the mainline. In terms of applying power to valve gears operation, the system is as simple as that.

**Hydraulic Locking**

Steam is actually a colourless gas, and the fluffy white stuff we see at the chimney is water droplets forming a dense cloud.

***Opposite**: The principals and design of valve gear and reverser were identical on both the original 'Merchant Navy' and 'West Country' designs. The valve gear was identical. The drawing is from a booklet produced to assist crews and fitters in understanding the operation of the gear. Below is what might well be called 'valve gear in a box'. We know it is the Bulleid type and may well have been a wooden mock-up produced to be shown to the various depots again as an aid to understanding.*

*In full flight and working as it should, apparently with steam to spare, 21C16 speeds along with what may well be a West of England or Bournemouth line working - judging by the one route disc that can be seen.*

*R K Blencowe collection*

Gases are compressible, and this means that any re-active forces coming back from the valve gear itself, as it oscillates back and forth, will push the piston in the cylinder back against the steam pressure. These oscillating forces can be large and, again, the amount of clatter demonstrating this in the cab, from a direct linked manual system when there is wear in the linkages of the valve gear, can be large. In addition, once the steam is shut off, it cools and condenses, and forms a partial vacuum, which can suck the piston back from its rest position. There is also the need to introduce an element of control so that, rather than powering the valve gear into full forward or reverse as the steam pushes the power piston to the ends of the cylinder, it can be locked in position part way so that the expansive properties of steam can be used to operate efficiently. This is commonly called "linking up" when applied to the valve gear and shuts the steam supply to the cylinders off part way through the piston stroke, to allow it to deliver power by expansion.

Liquids tend to be incompressible, or very nearly so. Use can be made of this property to hydraulically lock the power piston in any position, once the driver is satisfied that he has the right gear setting for the operating conditions of the moment. To achieve this, a second cylinder with its own piston mounted on the power piston rod, is rigidly fixed to the power cylinder casing. This cylinder is filled with oil, and the two ends of the cylinder are connected together via a pipe so that the oil can easily flow from one end to the other and back again as the power piston moves back and forth in its cylinder. A dead stop valve operable from the cab is fitted in the connection pipe. If this is closed, no oil can flow, and because the oil is incompressible, the locking piston becomes fixed. This then fixes the power piston rod, which is attached to the valve gear directly, hence fixing the valve setting.

The driver now has the facility of being able to operate the power piston to a position, and then by closing the hydraulic stop valve, effectively fixing the power piston and hence the valve gear in position. Provided this valve remains shut, no further linking up of the valve gear is possible.

**Control From The Cab**

There are now two elements of the power operating system that need to be controlled from the cab; the steam power operating cylinder and the hydraulic locking cylinder. In the Bulleid system, the same control lever is used to operate both parts of the system. The steam cylinder is fed with steam via a simple slide or D valve, exactly the same in principle as the slide valve used in the engine cylinders on some locomotives. The valve is moved backwards and forwards over the valve ports by a simple lever in the cab. This lever is organised to give sensible relative movements between what the driver does and what the locomotive does. He pushes the lever forward to move the locomotive forward, and pulls it backwards to move the locomotive backwards. The valve opening can be graduated to give a slow to fast operation, but as will be described later, the oil locking cylinder can be used to control the speed of movement of the steam power cylinder.

The slide valve performs two functions simultaneously. As it is moved across the port, it opens the pressure side of the power piston to steam and at the same time the non power side is opened to exhaust, allowing the piston to move and hence altering the valve setting. When the desired setting is achieved, the valve is moved to its central position where both ports are cut off from both steam and exhaust. The power piston is nominally now in equilibrium, and the valves are set. However, because the steam in the cylinders is compressible, cooling and condensing, the cylinder is in fact able to drift to any other equilibrium point it can find. This is obviously unacceptable, especially as a reversed position is possible, giving quite interesting results to the engines progress! In fact, it is most likely to fly into full gear, something the original Bulleid design has been accused of doing from time to time. It is at this point that the locking cylinder comes into play.

The hydraulic locking valve has two positions, open or closed. This is a simple rotating two ported plug valve. Using the same lever in the cab as is used to control steam admission to the power cylinder, the drive can operate the hydraulic valve by rotating the handle, thus opening and closing it. The valve linkage is driven off of a squared section of the operating shaft, lifting or dropping a link to the valve stem.

Further control of the power piston movement can be had by throttling the oil flow between the two ends of the hydraulic cylinder. A simple restriction in the pipe will achieve this, and in fact the driver has some control over this by not turning the control handle enough to fully open the locking valve, thus restricting the flow.

**To operate the gear**

The driver now has full control of the steam reversing gear. To operate from any given setting, he rotates the control handle to open the hydraulic valve, allowing oil to flow freely between both ends of the locking piston. He next moves the control handle backwards or forwards according to the valve movement he requires, and when the valve is in the correct position, he puts the lever back into the central position, shutting off the steam to both ends of the power piston, and rotates the control handle back to shut the hydraulic valve. The reversing gear in now locked in the new position.

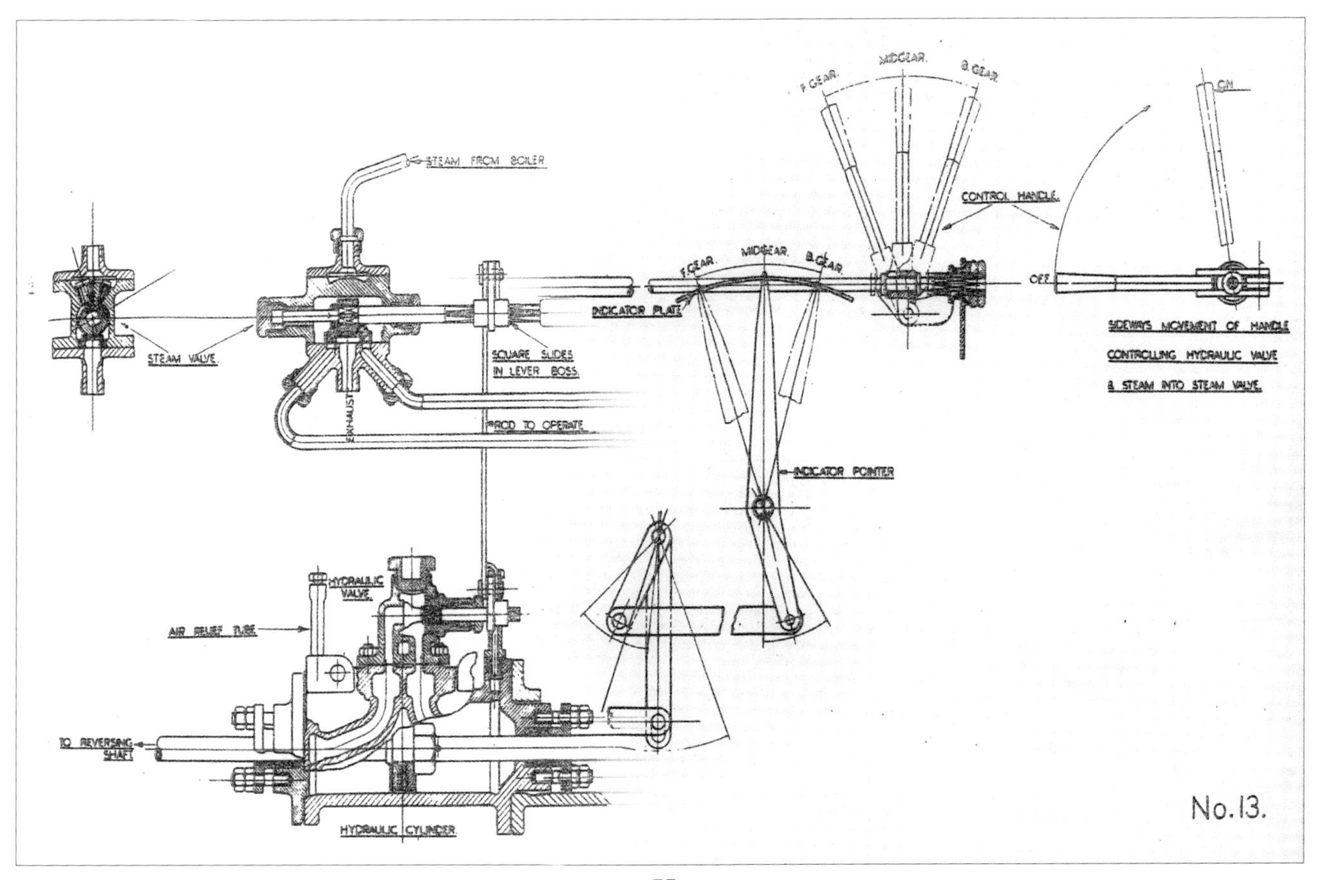

*External variations amongst the class.* ***Above*** *is the doyen 21C1 'Channel Packet', still with gunmetal plates and recorded at Exmouth Junction .* **Below** *No 35020 'Bibby Line' has a modified cab, cut down tender and extra long smoke deflectors. By this time, also, a replacement centre driving axle had been fitted, following the Crewkerne incident of the previous year. Notice also the engine retains its speed recorder fitting, 35020 having been the spare engine of the class during the 1948 interchange trials.* *R K Blencowe collection*

*The original Bulleid cab, prior to the sides raves being turned inwards to reduce the incident of drafts. Whilst this was certainly effective, it did create a working environment which was at times rather warm for comfort. No less than 140° being recorded in 1950.*

**Indication in the cab of the valve setting**

The use of the control handle gives no indication to the driver as to the valve setting he has achieved, and a separate method of giving him this information is required. On the Bulleid system, this is easily obtained by extending the power piston rod out of the power cylinder at the opposite end to the valve gear connection, and via a linkage to an indicator in the cab. To some extent, this negates the advantage of being able to physically position the operating system independently from the control, because the linkage is mechanical and fixed. Because it is only an indication though, the linkage is lightly constructed and able to follow a convenient route.

The linkage is again constructed so that the relationship between the sense of direction of the locomotive and the indicator is maintained, and is directly linked to the valve setting by means of the power piston rod. The driver now has a clear indication of the setting of the valve, and has full control over its positioning and locking.

**Some comments on the system**

The literature talks about the many problems of the original Bulleid design, including the valve gear problems. When one looks at the power reverser design, it is difficult to see how some of these comments arise.

One comment refers to the gear flying into full forward at times. The hydraulic locking cylinder cannot allow that to happen under normal operation. What could happen is that the oil system is allowed to empty, so that it cannot lock the piston rod in position, as it would have air in it which is compressible. Hence the locking fails to operate. This can only happen if the correct maintenance is not carried out, oil levels maintained and any air bled off via the air relief tube. The cab operating handle has to be positively rotated to open the locking valve, as the linkage is fixed to the operating shaft on a squared section. This is highly unlikely to happen by accident. The only other obvious possibility is that the locking piston becomes detached from the piston rod. This would result in a complete failure of the locomotive, as the valve setting would be almost random. Wear in the valve might allow slow leakage, so that the valve setting could then creep. Again, lack of maintenance is the culprit and simple attention to the valve would correct it.

Another comment refers to the driver never

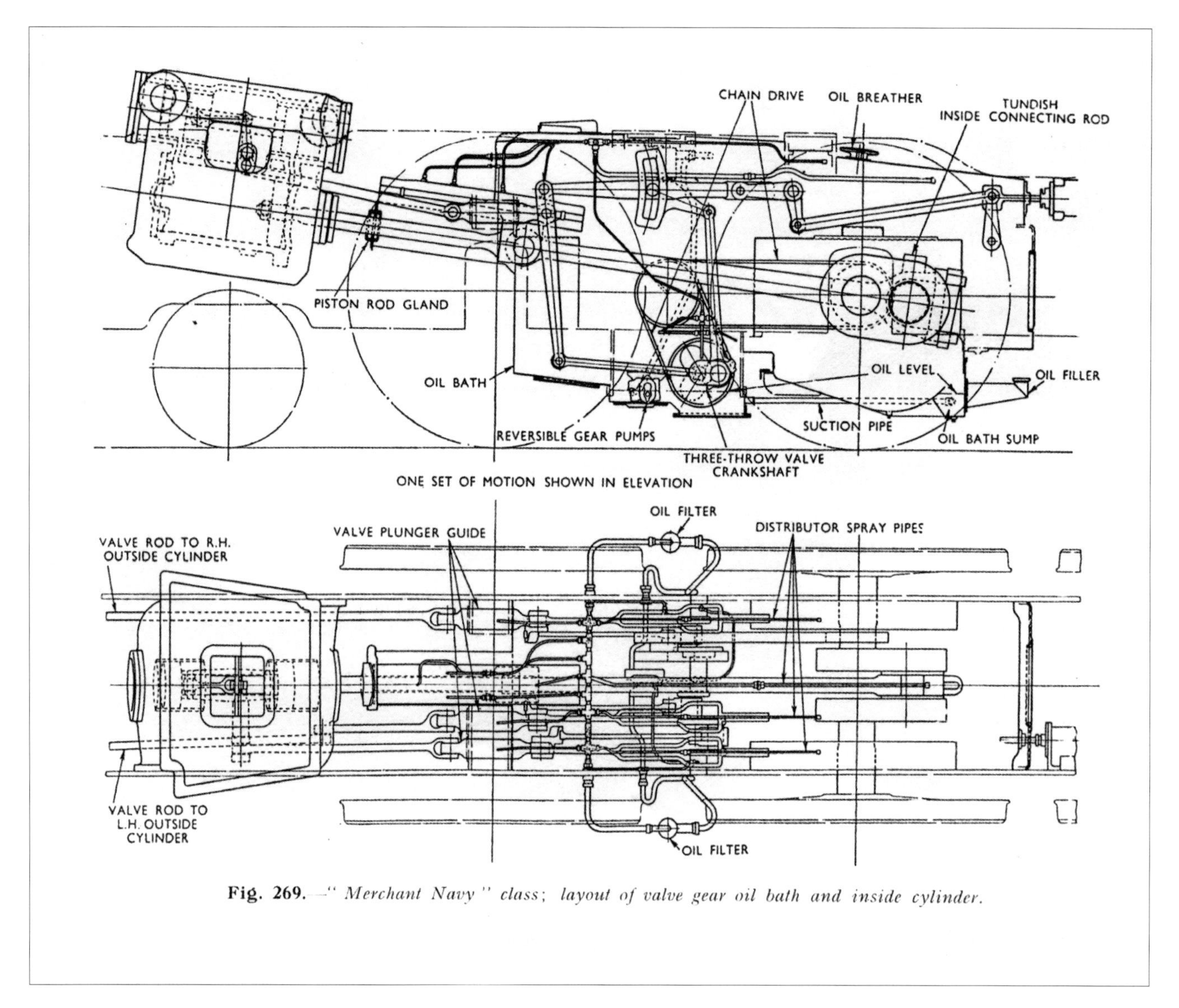


**Fig. 269.** *—" Merchant Navy " class; layout of valve gear oil bath and inside cylinder.*

knowing what the valve setting was. The indicator linkage is firmly attached to the power piston rod and the only way for this to fail is either though wear not being attended to in maintenance, or complete failure through breakage, in which case one would have thought the locomotive would have been failed on return to shed.

Comments have also been made about chain stretch invalidating the settings and the indications. Those chains were of massive construction, and anybody familiar with chain drives in general would know that even a 2% stretch is huge and is usually caused by wear in the pins and not by any stretching of the link material. It is difficult to see how wear in the whole of the valve gear drive could really make the indicator so far out as to be useless.

Having never driven an unrebuilt Bulleid, (firing one, though, is fun believe me), I cannot say if these comments are true or just legendary. Perhaps those who were lucky enough to work on these locomotives in steam days or current steam crews would like to comment on these matters.

Martin Breakspear is a Chartered Engineer by profession as well as an obvious railway enthusiast. He has offered us a number of fascinating technical explanations of matters relative to the Southern, with the next promised to be on the LSWR air-operated 'push-pull' system of working. Any relevant coach photographs to assist in illustrating this would be most welcome.

***Opposite, top:*** *Further variations in external appearance 21C10 'Blue Star', the lighter weight ribbed casing will be noted as with the obvious attempt at rounding the end of the smoke deflectors - see also cover view of 34035 some years later.*
***Opposite, bottom*** *- Evidence of a casing fire is all too apparent on 21C2 'Union Castle' in all too scruffy malachite green. This engine, too, is fitted with a speed recorder.*

SOUTHERN
21C10
21C10

21C2

*Permanent Way Notes by Graham Hatton*

# Third Rail Items on the Southern, Part 3 - Southern Conductor Rails.

The final part of this trio of articles discussing the conductor rail will examine items designed to provide electrical isolation of the power supply to sections of the track and items which provide a measure of safety to staff required to work on and around the conductor rail.

**Introduction**

The electrical supply to the conductor rail is transformed to the correct voltage at sub stations, which also house remotely operated circuit breakers to switch the supply to individual sections of track on or off. The circuit breakers also act as remotely re-settable fuses on the track supply cables and protect the railway and the electrical equipment in the event of a short circuit. On the open running line, sub stations tend to be four or five miles apart and a gap would be provided in the conductor rail adjacent to each sub station, therefore also splitting the conductor rail into sections approximately four or five miles long. A feed would be provided from the sub stations to the individual sections on either side, meaning that each section of conductor rail would have two separate supplies from adjacent sub stations.

The circuit breakers in the sub stations were worked from central control offices, of which there were a number around the Southern Region. These control centres were continuously manned, in much the same way as National Grid domestic supply control points are and operators could isolate sections of conductor rail between two sub stations remotely from these control centres. A diagrammatic panel with illuminated indicators also allowed the operators at these control centres to monitor the condition of the circuit breakers and hence the state of energization of any section of conductor rail in the area covered by each control centre.

This system of high speed circuit breaker, remote operation and control was expensive to install and the number of circuit breakers provided was therefore kept to the minimum practical level. Electrical feeds normally connected to one line, though this might emanate to more than one route, or would feed connected sidings. Parallel tracks were normally on separate circuit breakers. If isolation of a specific section of track was required for an engineering possession, it was accepted that track connected to the same electrical section would also become isolated and the design of track feeds would consider the isolation implications.

There are occasions where it is necessary to be able to isolate short specific sections of conductor rail, however, without isolation of the principal track electrical feed. For example, it may be necessary to be able to locally isolate the short length of conductor rail known as a 'floater', which can often be found adjacent to the section of a crossover, crossing the six-foot, between two parallel running lines. If it was left live when one of the two parallel tracks was under a track possession, with the required isolation for engineering work, it might present a greater risk to the unaware, due to its proximity to the line within the possession. Although conductor rail layout design tries to ensue that the collector shoes on a train, which are 'communed together', cannot bridge across an isolation gap, a similar situation can occur within junctions and short lengths of separately isolatable conductor rail can also be required here.

Only sidings which had to be accessible to electric stock were electrified, as the presence of a conductor rail poses a significant danger to yard shunters. Each siding from a common incoming track would often be separately isolatable on the ground, to allow repairs to track or trains, the supply being from an adjacent running line. In open electrified siding areas and in many sheds, where separate (trolley) feeds were not available, conductor rails were only extended part way into a shed or siding to ensure that a train was always in contact with a power feed but to limit the risk to staff.

In order to achieve local isolation of sections of conductor rail, or to switch alternative feeds for emergency use on or off, a mechanical switch was developed which could withstand the very high electrical current that would pass through it when a train started. This could be extremely high if the switch was situated at the entrance to a fan of sidings in which a train started, while all the other sidings were full of trains with their lights and heating on.

The switches were mechanical and locally worked by using a special insulated hook-ended switch pole, hence their universal name of 'hook switches'. There were many detail differences between the switches, but in general they consisted of a steel bar, clamped at both ends between two rotating threaded clamps which can clearly be seen in the photographs. The holes in the cranks could be caught with the hook ended pole to rotate the clamp mechanism and release the bar.

The first picture (above) of a recent hook switch shows the mechanics of the switch well. The conductor rail, raised above the running rail, is nearest the camera and the hook switch is mounted on it. It is not immediately obvious from this photograph, but the right hand end of the switch to which the substantial positive feed cable is attached is isolated from the conductor rail. The left hand end and clamping mechanism is fixed and electrically connected to the conductor rail so that when the rail is energised, so is the majority of the switch and pull levers on top. This hook switch is closed, i.e. power is passing from the cable through the switch to the rail. Opening the switch will electrically disconnect the cable from the rail by introducing an air gap between the two. The clamps are released by turning the levers to allow rotation of the bar, in this case around the left hand end, and retightened to prevent the switch rotating and shutting.

To indicate an open hook switch very often a red flag was placed in the lever hole of the open end. When closed everything is energised in the switch hence the need for an insulated (wooden) hook switch pole to operate the switch, as seen in the top picture overleaf. Earthing of the isolated rail is nowadays achieved separately .

**Opposite top -** By simply looking at the size of the cable attached to the previous photo, the size of the current involved passing through this switch can be judged! The switches evolved over the years as the current carried by such switches grew with greater consequent with power demands from new types of train.
The Southern Railway was concerned by the dangers these switches posed to staff operating them if they were operated poorly and commissioned a series of photos to illustrate good usage and the dangers of misuse. This is how to do it correctly! The hook switch operating pole is being correctly used and the man is standing some distance away from the switch and inclining his head away from any potential arc struck by an electrical load being applied across the switch. These days, the circuit breaker to the section of track which contains the hook switch, is often opened momentarily while the hook switch is operated, to remove the power supply and risk of any electrical arc from the switch.
In sidings, this is not always possible and an arc can still form, if a train on the section of track being isolated has an electrical fault, for instance, and is still drawing an electrical load. These photographs were taken in sidings, but the principal is the same as that used on the same switches fitted in running lines. The picture was also taken to illustrate the further danger of the proximity of a live conductor rail behind the legs of the man, a common feature with switches on running lines.

**Opposite bottom -** After having shown the correct method (and a series of photographs dealing with tight switches, which may have become partly welded shut, including the correct angle of the pole and head), the photographer turned his camera on how not to do it! This photograph demonstrates an incorrect stance. From this position, he has to push the switch open and if he slips while exerting force on the switch he could easily fall across the rails and come into contact with the live rail, despite the fact that the inside of the conductor rail is protected by a guard board.
A rail is often slightly slippery; more so if wet or oily. Hook switches should never, therefore, be pushed open across a rail but rather pulled open and then shut again. Note also the wooden protective trunking which was used for cables at this time. This has now fallen out of favour, but it did provide good protection to the cables from physical damage, especially in sidings or crossing tracks. On top of the trunking is the hook switch number.
All switches were numbered and referred to in conversations with the central controller in a carefully controlled and recorded sequence when the switches were opened. The white guard board ends were a final reminder to staff where no protection existed or where it ended and hence danger lurked. Conductor rail ends were sometimes also painted white to further reduce the risk to staff, particularly at night in depots and yards, but this wasn't universal. No doubt in war time blackouts, any additional highlighting would have been greatly appreciated by staff working in very difficult conditions. (Notice one deference between the two views that has evidently escaped the planning of the official photographer, in the top view the railwayman is not wearing gloves. Were the pole wet under these circumstances, the results could well have been fatal.)

**Overleaf -** A photograph taken at East Croydon station, again as one of a series of photographs illustrating the never ending and important tasks associated with maintaining guard boarding. This was provided for two main reasons: to protect staff and to protect track circuit and other signalling equipment which might be attached to the adjacent rail. This equipment was not designed to withstand a direct short from a live conductor rail.
Both rails are generally used for traction current return to the sub station in plain track, and the integrity of this route is essential to a DC electrification system. However, sometimes only one rail was used for this purpose and the other rail used for signalling reasons principally around switch and crossing work. In this instance the rails needed protection from shorts which might try and find an earth return through low voltage relays, far from improving them in the process!
Guard boarding is removable and therefore wasn't screwed directly to the brackets, but held upright a small distance (about 2 inches at the top) from the conductor rail by cleats which slide onto the brackets. These cleats are screwed to the guard boarding by very thick (No 14) short screws as the boarding, typically 1 3/8 inches thick and up to 9 foot long, does not allow much length for the screws to grip the wood, and they cannot project on the boards' inside edge.
The boarding was raised slightly above the conductor rail, but being wood and of considerable length between joints, it expands and contracts with the seasons. Properly installed and maintained this wasn't a problem, but maintenance often slipped and the screws worked loose. This was exacerbated by the 'gentle' removal techniques employed by the Permanent Way staff, which usually consisted of bars and size 12 boots. If the fixings were loose it would usually remain upright and dropped within the brackets, but not in its correct lateral position, hence it would be in danger of being struck by a passing shoe.

The boarding was cut around items attached to the conductor rail such as cables and hook switches, although this often severely compromised its strength, as this picture was taken to illustrate. The photograph again shows the cable entering trunking to pass under the foot crossing where a gap has been provided in the conductor rail.
Considerable interest is being shown by the seated passengers in the photographer's antics!

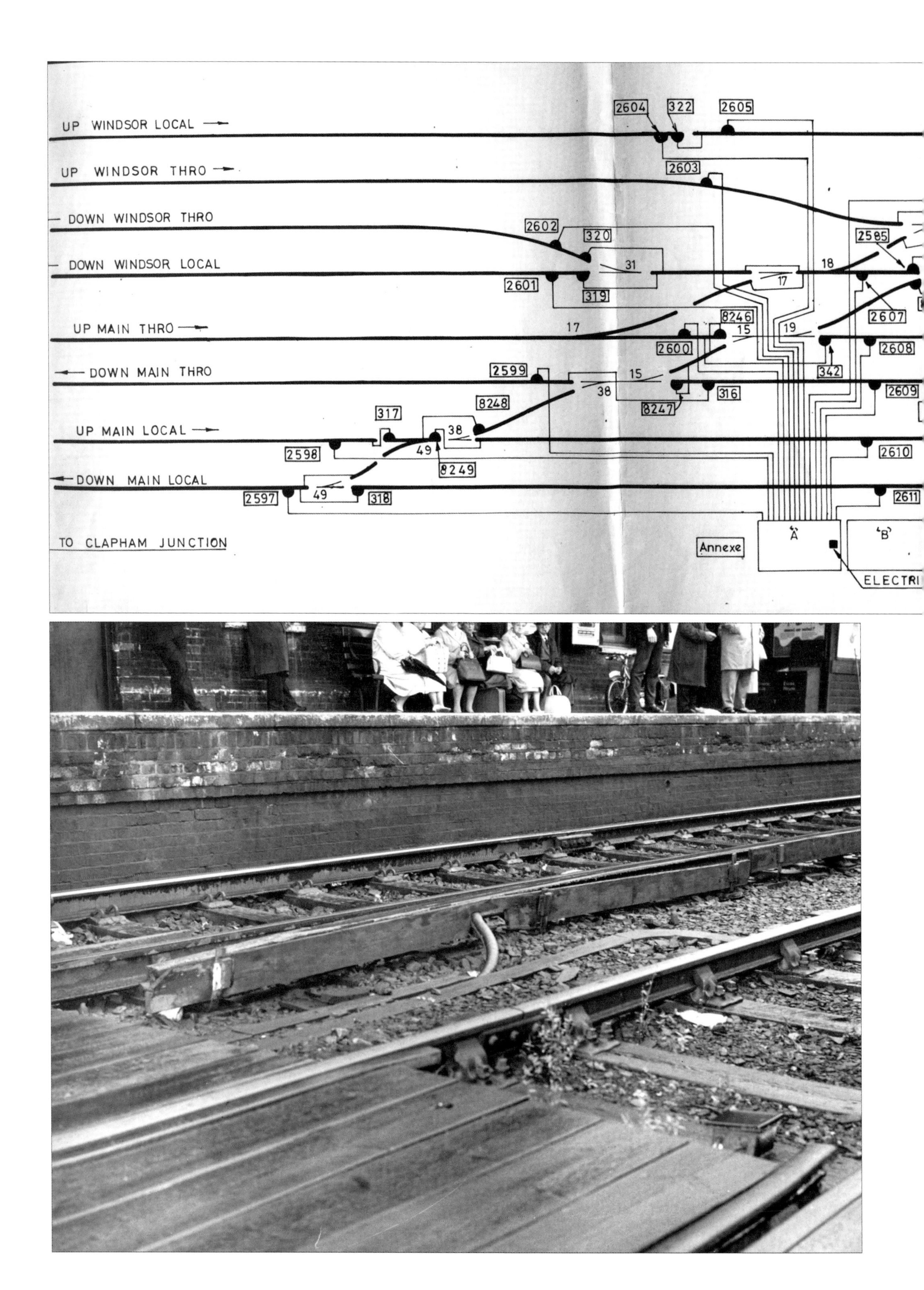

UP WINDSOR LOCAL
UP WINDSOR THRO
DOWN WINDSOR THRO
DOWN WINDSOR LOCAL
UP MAIN THRO
DOWN MAIN THRO
UP MAIN LOCAL
DOWN MAIN LOCAL
TO CLAPHAM JUNCTION
2604
322
2605
2603
2602
320
31
2601
319
2585
18
17
2607
8246
15
19
2600
2608
2599
342
38
316
2609
8248
8247
317
2598
49
8249
2610
2597
318
2611
Annexe
'A'
'B'
ELECTRI

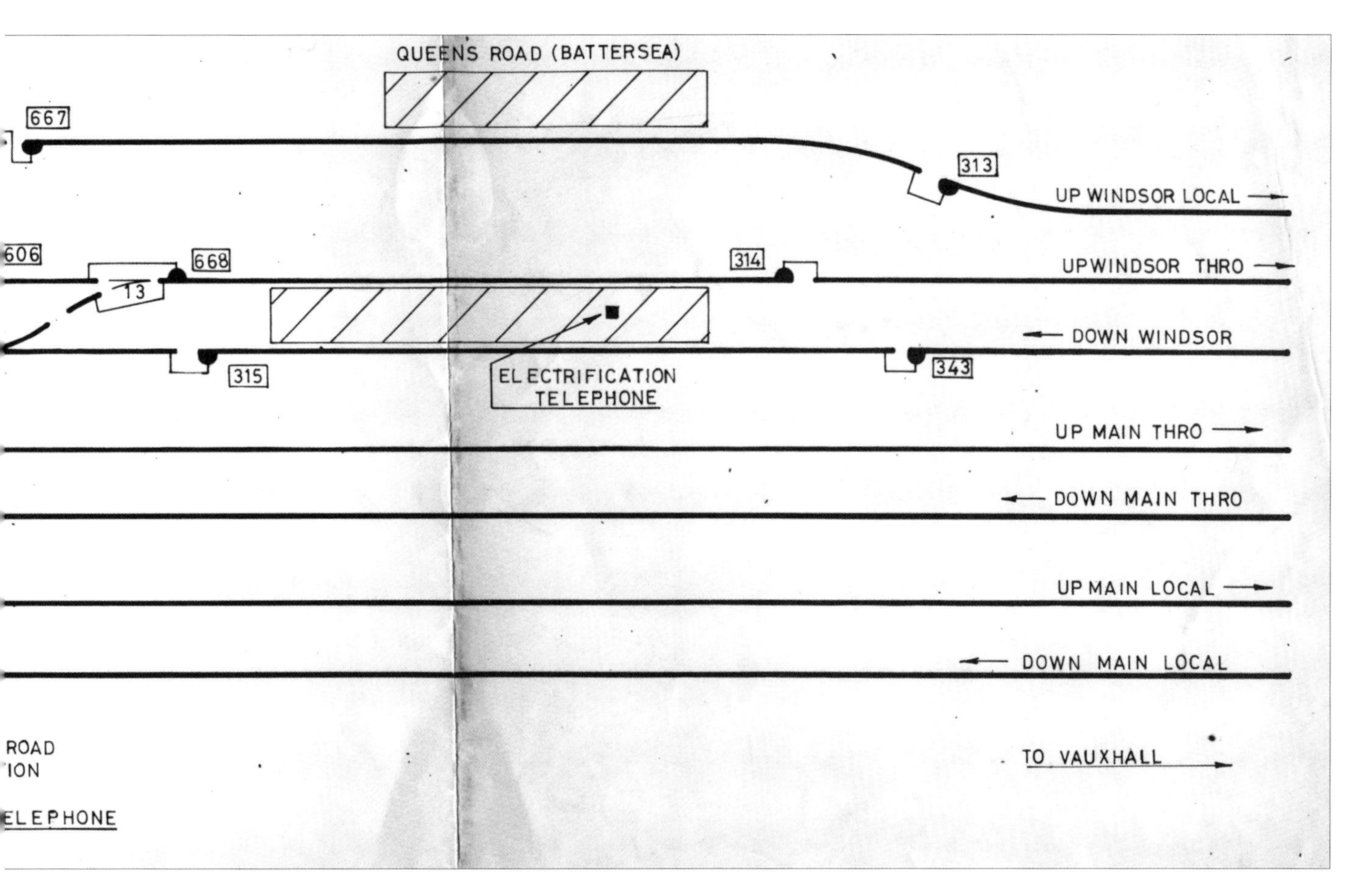


**Above: Diagram of Hook switches for Conductor Rail isolation as at Queen's Road, November 1973.**

"Supplementary instructions - Reference Electrified Lines Instructions Nos 21 and 29. Note: All messages must be repeated back to the sender.

To cut off current from conductor rail, telephone control operator at Raynes Park electrical control room using the electrification telephone. Give your name, grade, station where speaking from. Ask for current to be switched off stating line or lines affected and location and reason for doing so. Remain by the telephone until the electrical control operator tells you that the current is cut off or gives other directions.

The Electrical Control Operator will tell you which hook switch or hook switches, if any, to open or close and the order in which they are to be operated. No other switches must be operated. Switches must be opened or closed in the order given. Inform the electrical control operator immediately you have done so. Hook switches must never be operated without definite instructions from the electrical control operator.

To restore current to the conductor rails, telephone the electrical control operator and ask him to restore current to the conductor rails and await his instructions. Open or close any hook switches which the electrical control operator tells you to operate. Inform the electrical control operator immediately you have done so.

When current has been cut off from the conductor rails by means of a short circuiting bar and you are requested to ask for the current to be switched on, telephone the appropriate electrical control operator and ask him to restore the current, obtain and give the electrical control operator any details he may request.

The person asking for the current to be cut off becomes the man in charge of the isolation and the duty should not be transferred to any other person before notifying the electrical control operator the name of the person to whom it is being transferred.

All hook switches are numbered and are located at, near, or between fixed features shown on the diagram. The station manager must ensure that all his staff concerned are acquainted with the actual location of hook switches which they may be called upon to operate."

# FEEDBACK ON GEORGE HEIRON

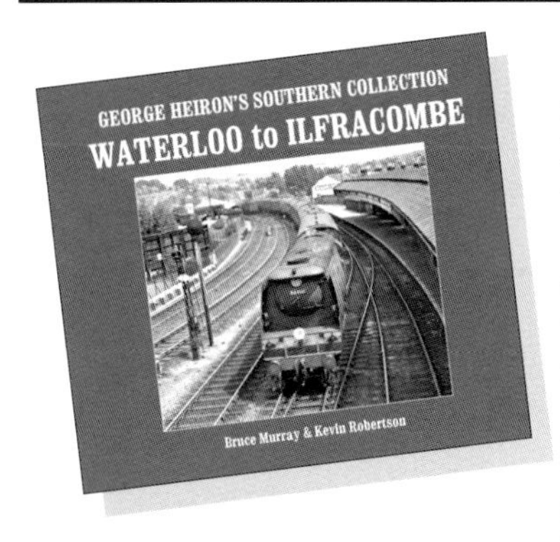


As referred to in the introduction, it had been intended to utilise this page for a 'catch-up' on letters and comments - and then this wonderful note arrived.

Both Bruce Murray and I are most grateful to Barry Sumsion for his comments and it did not take much to agree to his suggestion that they are included below. It just goes to show how useful is local knowledge.

"Dear Mr Robertson

"I have just received your publication 'Waterloo to Ilfracombe' featuring George Heiron's photographs. What a wonderful book! As a young boy and teenager, I was 'corrupted' in Salisbury. When off school with the 'flu', my parents knew to telephone the station if I was missing from my bed. Many were the times my name was called over the Tannoy. The pictures in this book of Salisbury in particular, bring back many happy memories. I am however one of those people who wish George had recorded times and dates. It does, though, give me pleasure at guessing some probable additions / information regarding some of the pictures. If I may be so bold then, may you find some of the following interesting if nothing else.

"The picture on page 18 right refers to something taking place at the front of the engine. Although I cannot possibly know for sure, it was not uncommon for the train reporting number to be changed at Salisbury. With what appears to be the Guard or other official 'supervising'. That would be my guess.

"Page 21's picture of 35009 leaving platform 2, reference is made to Nine Elms duty 28. From having watched these boards being replaced or not, we should not take too much heed of what the engine is carrying. Sorry about that but sometimes they changed them, sometimes not – they were obviously sometimes just forgotten, it being much more important to bring coal forward in the tender and to top up the water and oil round. 35009 was at that time a Salisbury engine, not moving away until rebuilt, and would not normally be heading the up ACE. It was probably a summer Saturday when the ACE ran in several portions, which this probably was.

"Page 24 lower: From the condition of the engine, (early tender crest and 'streamlining' missing ahead of the cylinders) I believe this was during the period when 34055 was a Salisbury engine. Again please do not take too much notice of the 'SPL' on the headcode disc. This was probably just an extra as suggested above.

"Page 24: I never heard what was platform 1 referred to as the up local line. It was used mostly by trains arriving from the western region and at busy times when platform 2 was occupied. Platform 6, over to the right, was more properly called a local platform, being the departure point for stopping Southampton / Portsmouth and Bournemouth line trains. 34047 was a Brighton engine and my guess is that it had just taken over a Brighton train. Since the leading coach is a Bulleid one (and not a WR one) and another pacific can be seen ahead in the waiting siding, (which probably arrived with the train from the west) this is probably a Plymouth-Brighton train. This would normally have used platform 2 but occasionally used platform 1.

"Page 26 lower: These two Bulleid pacifics are in the waiting siding. Engines sometimes came off the shed in twos and threes and ran light engines coupled together to await their trains. They are probably being uncoupled. I cannot remember two pacifics ever double-heading east from Salisbury. 34044 was a Bournemouth engine and probably has worked up from Bournemouth (perhaps double heading with a T9 or U) on a train from Bournemouth the previous evening. I am guessing that this will be for a Saturday extra off the Western Region to the Bournemouth neck of the woods. Frequently trains would come from the Welsh valleys with 'Holiday Expresses' bound for the south coast. There was no balancing working until the following Saturday when everyone went home. Salisbury shed then sent anything up to five or six western engines back light towards Westbury and beyond, all coupled together only to return a week later!

"Page 27: Again do not take too much notice of what is shown on the board. Apart from having a Waterloo line headcode, Eastleigh bound trains would normally have left from platform 1 or 6.

"Page 32 right: Again unusual for a MN to be in platform 1. Notice also that this was the time when French Line was fitted with a single chimney.

"Page 39 upper: I would bevery surprised to discover that the photograph was not taken from 'Gramshaw Road foot crossing'. This is part of a footpath leading from the main A30 (on the left) to the road through the village of Bemerton which by now had become part of Salisbury.

"I hope that the above observations will not in any way cause offence. It's just that this book has fired my nostalgia like no other. Please let's have some more. Put them in 'The Southern Way' if you have to, I'm a regular of that also."

*I am sure I speak for many when I record, thank you - KR.*

# ACCIDENTS AND EMERGENCIES AT GUILDFORD

Pick up almost any issue of the erstwhile *SOUTHERN RAILWAY MAGAZINE* for the period 1923-47 and one common feature is the page, or pages, devoted to Ambulance issues, under the auspices of what was then referred to as the St John Ambulance Association.

The railway company, not just the SR of course, encouraged staff to become members of the St John Association, this an age when medical facilities were limited and the ambulance service which we take for granted today, was still many years into the future. Accordingly staff were trained to deal with almost any emergency that might arise and ranging from the number of casualties that might well occur consequent upon a major accident to lesser, almost daily, injuries to both staff and indeed passengers. As indicated, the issues of the SR Magazine would feature the results of competitions between various stations and depots, that for example of March 1933, referring to 113 teams, involving 565 members, having entered the competitions. Awards were presented to both the women's and men's teams by Sir Herbert Walker and Mrs Szlumper. Guildford at the time was in District No2 and had an 'A', 'B', and 'C' team, as well a 'Beginners 'D' team. So far as the St John Association was concerned, Guildford Station was part of their No VIII district.

There, at least, is a very brief record of an almost forgotten aspect of the SR and where matters might be expected to rest, little more perhaps than a space filler of a few lines. Except, that is, for an approach and meeting with Peter Holt in 2007. Peter is a retired railwayman, who spent some time at Guildford where, when the station was being rebuilt, he managed to save a few items of local history which would otherwise have been consigned to oblivion. Amongst these was the Guildford Station St John Ambulance Association 'Occurrence Book', covering incidents at the station between May 1931 and February 1934. Herein each incident is recorded with a consecutive number but with little more than a line of detail. The record commences with;

| Case No | Date | Name of Person Injured | Address | Nature of Injury | By Whom First aid was rendered | How treated and whither removed | Result | Doctor's Endorsement and Remarks when possible |
|---|---|---|---|---|---|---|---|---|
| 926 | 16/5/1931 | Underman Idlaw | Guildford | Cut forehead | Sgt. Burgess | Cleansed and dressed | | |

There follows what well be expected to be a long and of course for the unfortunate victim, often painful list of cuts, bumps, burns, sprains and bruises, mainly at times seemingly affecting railwaymen of all grades and from all departments, but with the names of passengers also appearing at intervals. One fatality was also recoded during the period, a steamraiser, who was scalded to death. Note also the First Aider's title is given in accordance with St John rankings, rather than the grade of the railwayman themselves. A few lesser incidents however stand out, both concerning passengers and which today may perhaps raise a wry smile, not only so far as the treatment offered, but also concerning the traffic dealt with at Guildford. They are as follows:

| 1086 | 14/8/1932 | Mr Weadon | Manor Farm Cottages Claygate | Bitten by a Bear | Pte. W R White | Wound cleansed and dressed | | |
|---|---|---|---|---|---|---|---|---|
| 1285 | 26/8/1933 | Mrs Vigors | Stations Cottages, Effingham | Wasp sting on tongue | Pte. Paverley | Slice of raw onion in mouth until pain ceased. | | Treatment satisfactory – Dr Smith said. |
| 1336 | 31/10/1933 | Shunter Paverley | Effingham | Electric Shock | Pte. Paverley | Salvolatile *(smelling salts!)* and water. | | |
| 1374 | 3/1/1934 | Mr Johnson | Effingham | Dog bite on leg | Pte.. Paverley | Cleansed and dressed. | | |

It may well be that the Guilford book covered occurrences at various outstations for as can be seen Effingham is also referred to. The dog bite incident was in fact the second reference to the same happening at the same location. A Mr Daw having been treated and dressed by Pte. Blundy on 5$^{th}$ August 1932.

Some staff also appeared to be what would be referred to as accident prone, the name of Miss Wells from the Refreshment Department appearing no less than three times in the space of less than two years, whilst both the Assistant Station Master and Station Master also feature, the latter twice. There were also entries for the staff from the W H Smith bookstall as well as Taxi Drivers and Carters. Health and Safety may not, perhaps, have been particularly well established eighty years ago, although to compensate for this the number of willing and capable staff at hand in the event of an incident was hopefully a reassurance.

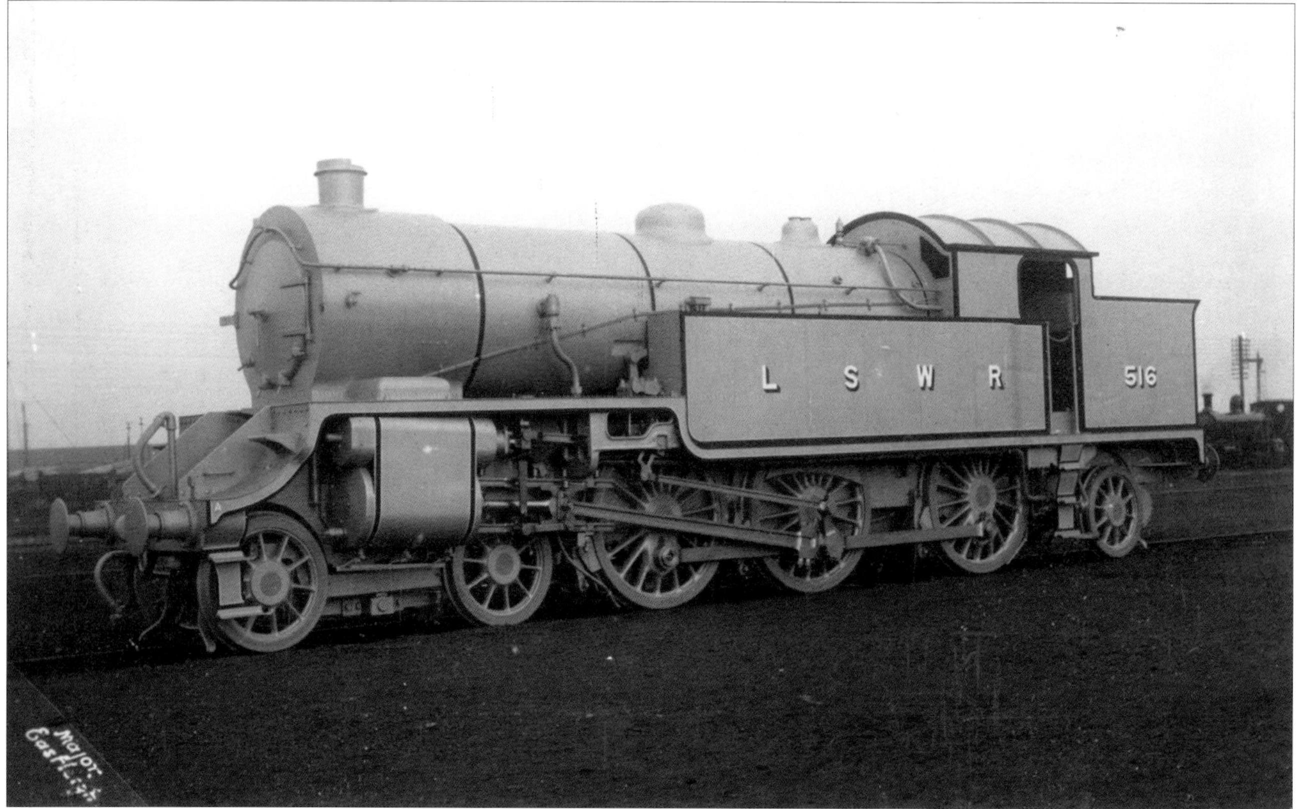


*Works grey views of the first member of each of type, recorded outside the front of Eastleigh Works in July 1921 and November 1921 respectively. Notice in both cases the care taken in positioning the locomotives with the rods 'down'. The rudimentary safety-chain across the cab opening will be noted. The name of 'Major-Eastleigh' obviously refers to the photographer, known to have been a local man employed by the railway as required. His collection was still extant until comparatively recent years but has since disappeared - any suggestions would be most welcome!*

# URIE'S BIG TANKS

ERIC YOULDON

## G16 class:

In 1921 the LSWR completed these four 4-8-0 tanks at Eastleigh to Urie design. Numbered 492 – 495 they were put to work on hump shunting at Feltham and short distance goods trains in the London area. Typical Urie design was followed, but the boiler was smaller than on his 4-6-0 classes and in fact was based on that on the Drummond D15 4-4-0.

The G16s were a success, although doubts were expressed over the wisdom of incorporating a superheater in a locomotive for this class of work. In 1922 No 493 was given trials at Eastleigh, Salisbury, Exmouth Junction and Bournemouth and four more were ordered (without superheater) but not built. In 1927 any further expansion of the class was forgotten when Maunsell drew up his 'Z' class 0-8-0 for heavy shunting.

SR livery was initially black with thin green lining but from around the mid-thirties, lining was dropped. The introduction of diesel shunters saw the demise of the class and they were withdrawn in 1959 (30492 and 30493) and late 1962 (30494 and 30495).

## H16 class:

The H16 class of 4-6-2 tanks totalling five were built at Eastleigh in 1921-22 and numbered 516-520. Design was generally similar to the G16 class – boilers in particular were interchangeable – and their main employment, again from Feltham shed, was on transfer goods around London plus short distance passenger work. These big tank engines successfully and reliably carried

*G16 No 495 at Feltham in as new condition. The familiar loco shed and tower are visible in the background. The size and weight of the new engines meant there were no less than 11 occasions when one of the four new engines 'fell-off' within the yard during September / October 1921. The loco is at the head of what appears to be a lengthy train and is displaying the headcode for a service to Willesden.*

*30518 at Feltham on 27th October 1962 displays the later modifications. Cover above cylinder removed; automatic warning system added of which the battery box under the bunker is shown, overhead warning flashes on frame and firebox; top lamp iron lowered. Plain slidebars, unique to this H16 can be discerned.* *RAS Marketing*

out their tasks which in due course included regular appearances at Waterloo on empty stock workings. New ground was broken when, having been replaced by diesels around London, 30516/7 were transferred to Eastleigh in January 1960 for hauling heavy oil tank trains over the Fawley branch. These were followed by 30518-20 in January 1961. Residence in Hampshire proved to be short lived when 'W' class 2-6-4 tanks took their place and all the H16s were back at Feltham by May 1961. Little work remained for the class and all five were taken out of service in late 1962; the last recorded operation being performed by 30517 on a railtour on December 16th 1962.

The SR livery for the H16s was lined passenger green until 1940 when 519 became plain light green. After this unlined black was the order of the day, relieved only by 30520's treatment, detailed later.

**Detail variations:**

No drastic modifications were accorded the nine big tanks, even their stovepipe chimneys (later without capuchons) and LSWR smokebox doors survived to the end. Maunsell superheaters superseded the Eastleigh variety with attendant snifting valves, although these valves were removed in the late 1940s. Cab roof ventilators were introduced by the Southern. No 518, around 1946, had its fluted slidebars replaced by plain type but no others had this change. Nos 30518 and 30520, when in Eastleigh Works in mid-1960, had the heavy raised cover removed each side on the platform above the cylinders, whence the opening was covered by a plain flat plate. This gave rise to the question: what had the hefty raised casting accommodated? Well, research revealed that the answer was – nothing! It was apparently no more than an elaborate cover, almost ornamental, for an opening in the platform. However, in an odd sort of way it enhanced appearance and 30518/20 looked slightly lost without it. These two in 1960 became AWS equipped.

In final days, when we were all more aware of the spread of overhead conductors, G16s 30494 and 30495 and all the H16s had the front top lamp iron lowered from the curved handrail to a position just above the smokebox numberplate. About the same time plastic warning flashes were attached to some engines on front of the tank, frame and rear of bunker.

**BR Liveries:**

All nine tanks entered BR service in January

***Opposite page*** *- Two views of members of the H16 class at Strawberry Hill, Nos 517 and 519, both clean but No 519 seemingly superb. The position of the toolbox on the front framing and which was common to both types of tank engine, will be noted.*

517
L S W R

519
L S W R

1948 in unlined black with numbers and SOUTHERN, all in that company's sunshine style. What follows is a survey of changes in BR service although plain black continued to be the basic livery except where indicated.

SS – refers to 'sunshine style'.

GS – refers to 'Gills Sans'.

The first crest (lion and wheel) was applied in the small size unless shown otherwise, whilst the second crest was applied in the small version only.

SNP – smokebox numberplate added.

| | BR Number / Livery | Notes |
|---|---|---|
| 30492 | 12/48 SS | Retained Southern. SNP 9/50 number in GS. 2/53 $1^{st}$ crest. |
| 30493 | 9/48 in GS | British Railways in GS. SNP. 5/50 $1^{st}$ crest. |
| 30494 | 2/48 as s494 in SS | British Railways in SS. 9/50 renumbered 30494 in GS. SNP. 7/52 number in GS. $1^{st}$ crest. C4/59 $2^{nd}$ crest. |
| 30495 | 5/48 in SS | British Railways in SS. 12/49 number in GS. $1^{st}$ crest in large size. SNP. 2/52 $1^{st}$ crest small size. 4/58 $2^{nd}$ crest. |
| 30516 | 9/49 in GS | $1^{st}$ crest SNP. 7/57 $2^{nd}$ crest. |
| 30517 | 7/48 in GS | British Railways in GS. SNP. 1/51 $1^{st}$ crest. 10/60 $2^{nd}$ crest. |
| 30518 | 11/50 in GS | SNP. $1^{st}$ crest. |
| 30519 | 4/49 in GS | Blank tanks. SNP. 6/52 $1^{st}$ crest. |
| 30520 | 11/48 in GS | British Railways in GS. SNP. Lined black. 10/51 $1^{st}$ crest, lining discarded. 11/57 $2^{nd}$ crest. |

All dates are ex Eastleigh Works.

30520's lined black livery was a one-off special; the loco was expected to be dedicated to Waterloo empty stock workings and therefore warranted special treatment.

Some of the above appeared in the Urie Society's Newsletter in 2005.

*Southern livery for No 494. Despite the fact the G16 were supposedly restricted more to shunting rather than trip working, the final mileage for the two classes were not considerably different, being in the order of 800,000 to 950,000.*

***Top*** *- Empty stock working for an unidentified member of the H16 class, still in SR livery but possibly recorded very early into the BR period.*

*Arthur Tayler*

***Centre*** *- 30517 at Clapham Junction on 27th August 1948, shortly after having received its smokebox numberplate and ownership wording - see table opposite. Due to several derailments of the rear pony truck, bunker first running into Waterloo by the class was prohibited shortly afterwards. Sister engine, No 30519, was noted on similar ecs duties the following month.*

*Arthur Tayler*

***Bottom*** *- 30494 outside the rear of Eastleigh shed on 9th September 1961, just 15 months away form withdrawal. At this stage, available work for the two remaining members of the 4-8-0 type, Nos 30494 and 30495 was limited, their work at Feltham having been taken over by diesels. The electrification warning flash will be noted. One final point of note is that the cab of the 4-8-0T was narrower compared with the 4-6-2T. The reason for this was to allow the driver to stand outside, useful when shunting, and still reach the regulator.*

*Tony Molyneaux*

## The Remembrance Class in detail

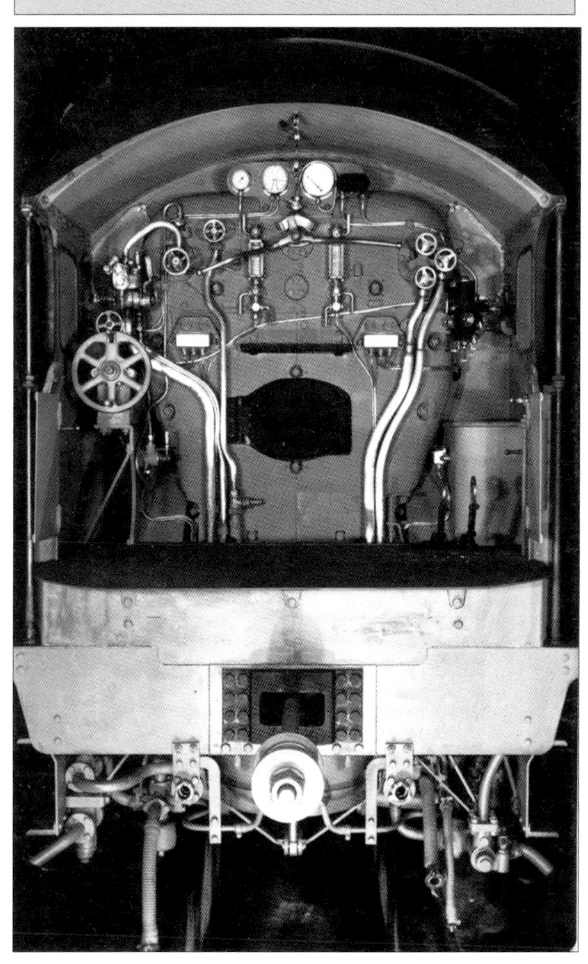

It is always pleasing to find something a little unusual or quirky to include in 'SW' and I have to confess that this one would certainly seem to fit the bill. Firstly, amongst a raft of material loaned to us from Howard Butler some time ago was the above view of No 2329 'Stephenson' unusually recorded inside Eastleigh works in the autumn of 1934 at the time of conversion from tank to tender engine. Next to arrive was this cab view of the class, undated but certainly from the same period. Finally, Eric Best alerted us to the colour spread opposite from the *RAILWAY MAGAZINE* of, we believe 1937. Although the circumstances were not explained at the time, clearly there was some internal discussion taking place with regard to future colour schemes, part of which is recounted by C F Klapper in his biography of Sir Charles Walker. It appears various senior Southern men felt a change of colour scheme might well attract passengers bookings and Klapper refers to the discussion concerning coaching stock. Evidently the 'RM' was bold enough to suggest the colours seen opposite as potential for locomotives. But returning to contemporary coaching stock, Klapper recounts a journey to the Isle of Wight made by Walker in the company of Maunsell, Cox and Bushrod, each respectively believing coaches should in future be painted, grey, or green with gold lining, or green all over. Walker took no part in the discussion but after lunch at Ryde, he, "went across to an optician's shop where reels of spectacle cord were displayed in the window. He dashed in, emerged quickly with a length of green cord, produced nail scissors, and cut off a piece for each of the officers. He still had an abundant part of the reel, 'Now, argument shall cease; that will be the colour Southern engines and coaches shall be painted in the future. This reel shall remain in my office safe as the standard to which reference shall be made.' When Bullied became responsible for the painting of Southern locomotives and coaches the choice of malachite green was thus made inevitable by a general manager, who had retired a fortnight before Bulleid's appointment began."

# COLOUR INTERLUDE

***This page***: *Travels with my camera -1. Barcombe Mills on the Uckfield line, 'Q' class 0-6-0 No 30549 employed on the daily goods working.*
***Opposite***: *Travels with my camera -2. Pre grouping survivor at Epsom Downs recorded in February 1971.*

*Gerald Daniels*

*Travels with my camera -3. This time the location is eastwards at Hailsham on the erstwhile 'Cuckoo Line'. The overhead electrification warning on the tender may once have been appropriate at the next station north Hellingly, reference the former Hospital Railway. The train is a down, southbound service, from Tunbridge Wells West to Eastbourne.*

*Gerald Daniels*

*Travels with my camera - 4. Closed season at Sandown, stored 'O2' locomotives in the spring, awaiting a return for the summer service. In the foreground is the trackbed of the former line to Merstone and Newport, closed in 1956. Nos 20 'Shanklin' and 30 'Shorwell' can be positively identified, with it is believed 31' Chale' at the end of the line. Trust and honesty prevailed at the time as all still retain their nameplates.* *Gerald Daniels*